Passing Game

A DRAMA IN TWO ACTS

By Steve Tesich

D0746660

No part of this book may be reproduced, stored in a retrieval system, or transmitted in any form, by any means, including mechanical, electronic, photocopying, recording, or otherwise, without the prior written permission of the publisher.

S A M U E L F R E N C H, I N C.
45 West 25th Street   NEW YORK, N.Y. 10010
7623 Sunset Boulevard   HOLLYWOOD 90046
LONDON   *TORONTO*

HOUSTON PUBLIC LIBRARY

RO1155 00947 78, BY Steve Tesich

ALL RIGHTS RESERVED

CAUTION: Professionals and amateurs are hereby warned that PASSING GAME is subject to a royalty. It is fully protected under the copyright laws of the United States of America, the British Commonwealth, including Canada, and all other countries of the Copyright Union. All rights, including professional, amateur, motion pictures, recitation, lecturing, public reading, radio broadcasting, television, and the rights of translation into foreign languages are strictly reserved. In its present form the play is dedicated to the reading public only.

PASSING GAME may be given stage presentation by amateurs upon payment of a royalty of Fifty Dollars for the first performance, and Thirty-five Dollars for each additional performance, payable one week before the date when the play is given to Samuel French, Inc., at 45 West 25th Street, New York, NY 10010; or at 7623 Sunset Blvd., Hollywood, CA 90046, or to Samuel French (Canada), Ltd., 100 Lombard Street, Toronto, Ontario, Canada M5C 1M3.

Royalty of the required amount must be paid whether the play is presented for charity or gain and whether or not admission is charged.

Stock royalty quoted on application to Samuel French, Inc.

For all other rights than those stipulated above, apply to Marian Searchinger Associates, Inc., 888 Seventh Avenue, 18th Floor, New York, N.Y. 10019.

Particular emphasis is laid on the question of amateur or professional readings, permission and terms for which must be secured in writing from Samuel French, Inc.

Copying from this book on whole or in print is strictly forbidden by law, and the right of performance is not transferable.

Whenever the play is produced the following notice must appear on all programs, printing and advertising for the play: "Produced by special arrangement with Samuel French, Inc."

Due authorship credit must be given on all programs, printing and advertising for the play.

Anyone presenting the play shall not commit or authorize any act or omission by which the copyright of the play or the right to copyright same may be impaired..

No changes shall be made in the play for the purpose of your production unless authorized in writing.

The publication of this play does not imply that it is necessarily available for performance by amateurs or professionals. Amateurs and professionals considering a production are strongly advised in their own interests to apply to Samuel French, Inc., for consent before starting rehearsals, advertising, or booking a theater or hall.

Printed in U.S.A.

ISBN 0 573 61443 1

THE AMERICAN PLACE THEATRE

Wynn Handman　　　　　**Julia Miles**
DIRECTOR　　　　　ASSOCIATE DIRECTOR

PRESENTS

PASSING GAME

by
STEVE TESICH

Directed by
PETER YATES

Set by　　　　　Costumes by
KERT LUNDELL　　　　　**RUTH MORLEY**

Lighting by
NEIL PETER JAMPOLIS

Basketball sequences choreographed by
RICHARD D. MORSE

CAST
(In Order of Appearance)

Debbie .... Susan MacDonald
Randy .... Paul C. O'Keefe
Richard .... William Atherton
Julie .... Margaret Ladd
Andrew .... Pat McNamara
Henry .... Howard E. Rollins Jr.
Rachel .... Novella Nelson

Setting: Upstate New York
Time: Present

Standbys—for Debbie and Julie: Jacklyn Lee Bartone; Henry: Dean Irby; Richard and Andrew: Barry Jenner; and Rachel: Cynthia McPherson

CAST

RICHARD, *actor, any age.*

JULIE, *his wife. Slightly younger.*

HENRY, *black actor. Richard's age.*

RACHEL, *Henry's wife. Julie's age.*

ANDREW, *night watchman.*

RANDY, *his young nephew.*

DEBBIE, *his girl friend.*

TIME

Present.

PLACE

Upstate New York.

Passing Game

ACT ONE

SCENE 1

HENNESSY *cottage.*

ANDREW *enters from* S. L. *He crosses to* D. C. *on the basketball court. He pauses, loads his shotgun and moves on. The stage is dark. It is night. A shot is heard in the distance.* RANDY *jumps up from the couch.* DEBBIE *runs out of the bedroom.*

DEBBIE. What was that?

RANDY. Sounded like Uncle Andrew's shotgun. He goes hunting at night sometimes. (*Light goes on in the Jefferson cottage and* HENRY *steps out.*)

HENRY. I don't see anybody. (DEBBIE *runs to the window and looks out at him.* RANDY *also looks over at him.*)

DEBBIE. I know him. I mean I've seen him on TV.

RANDY. Uncle says the guy who owns this place's been on TV too. He did some dogfood commercials or something.

HENRY. So what do you want me to do, Rachel? (HENRY *goes back inside.*)

RANDY. Want to go to the bedroom?

DEBBIE. Not now.

RANDY. What's the matter? You used to love to break into other people's cottages and goof around. (*Smells the perfume.*)

DEBBIE. Maybe I've changed.

RANDY. What did you do? Steal some of that lady's cologne?

DEBBIE. I did not.

RANDY. You used to love to steal little things.

DEBBIE. I just put some on. And it's perfume. Not cologne. Here smell.

RANDY. Did you do your breasts like you used to? (*He puts his nose in her cleavage.*)

DEBBIE. That's enough. C'mon. Take your damn nose out of there. (*She pushes him away and crosses to sofa and turns on flashlight.* RANDY *stops.*)

RANDY. The only way I ever got anything off you was to force you. A couple of times you even pretended to be drunk.

DEBBIE. I was drunk.

RANDY. No you weren't. I saw you spilling booze out of the car when you thought I wasn't looking.

DEBBIE. Cheat. (*She sits on sofa.*)

RANDY. (*He crosses to sofa and sits.*) I was hoping to get you pregnant. You never would've left for the city had I got you pregnant.

DEBBIE. Maybe not.

RANDY. And you wanted me to get you pregnant. Only it had to be by accident. Like it just happened somehow.

DEBBIE. You had your chance. It's too late now.

RANDY. But you did come back.

DEBBIE. Just to visit. See everyone . . . my parents' house.

RANDY. All the kids are gone. Your parents moved to Florida. I'm the only one left. So maybe you really came back to see me and give me another chance.

DEBBIE. I see you haven't changed at all.

RANDY. (*He takes her hand.*) Hmm. I'm not as sweet as I once was. I was as sweet as baby corn in those days. So, what brings you here if not me?

DEBBIE. (*She rises and crosses to door.*) I told you. Besides . . . it's very hot in the city.

RANDY. Must be hot for everybody. And yet the people who used to come up here got scared off.

DEBBIE. So?

RANDY. So, it must be hotter for you in the city than for most. (*He takes flashlight and shines it in her face.*) I mean to get you to come up.

DEBBIE. (*She crosses back toward him.*) Maybe I wanted to see if you still love me. (*She takes the flashlight out of her eyes.*)

RANDY. All you got to do is ask.

DEBBIE. I'm not going to ask.

(*A car is heard pulling up to the cabin.* RANDY *jumps up. Runs to the door and peeks out.*)

RANDY. It's the people. Let's get out of here. (*They exit together. Enter* RICHARD *and* JULIE.)

RICHARD. WELCOME. (JULIE *ignores him. Looks around.*)

JULIE. Quit stalling. You know what you have to do. (*Hands him a flyswatter.*)

RICHARD. I feel silly just thinking about it.

JULIE. All I'm asking for is a little commotion . . . a fair warning to any spiders, june bugs, centipedes and-a-, whoever else might be here . . . that we're back. (*He lifts up the rug, jumps and goes into a tap routine to Forty-second Street. Getting the beat going he starts into a little soft-shoe, very corny and self-conscious, from which he moves on to a much more wild free form choreography . . . a parody of sorts of Gene Kelly. Very show biz, he stops by flopping down on the sofa.*)

RICHARD. How was that?

JULIE. It should be a warning to them . . . to all of

us. (*She enters the kitchen and puts the groceries down on the table, and begins to sort through them.*) I don't know why we bought this stuff. We always assume that being in the country will give us an appetite for food we hate in the city. Pork and beans . . . corn meal mush . . . You'd think we were ashamed to bring a bagel into the woods.

RICHARD. Everything looks fine.

JULIE. Yes. The faucets are pouring forth . . . the fridge is fridging . . . the sink is sinking and the lights are lighting . . . your telephone is over there . . .

RICHARD. Yes, but it's not ringing.

JULIE. (*She puts entire bag of groceries in the refrigerator.*) I bet you get something tomorrow. Friday's your lucky day.

RICHARD. Since when?

JULIE. (*Pause.*) That's funny?

RICHARD. What?   .

JULIE. I thought I smelled that old perfume of mine.

RICHARD. Me too.

JULIE. (*She pulls out a chair and sits.*) Ah, a house in the country. There really should be somebody here to greet us.

RICHARD. Like in a Russian novel.

JULIE. Exactly. Parents . . . or grandparents . . .

RICHARD. (*He sits on the floor and puts his head on her lap.*) And an unmarried daughter who looks after them and says things like: You must tell me all about the city, you really must . . .

JULIE. Something like that . . . Wouldn't you like that, Rich.

RICHARD. I guess I don't have roots like you but, yes, I would like it . . . for your sake.

JULIE. Can I ask you a terrible question? (RICHARD *gets up and crosses to the suitcase.*)

RICHARD. That in itself is a terrible question.

JULIE. Why are we here?

RICHARD. Why are we here? According to Schopenhauer . . .

JULIE. I'm serious.

RICHARD. So is Schopenhauer. (*He exits to bedroom.*)

JULIE. I bet you expect me to run around and have fun up here.

RICHARD. You don't have to run around.

JULIE. (*She crosses U. L. slowly L. of pillar.*) Then I have to stand on the porch with my hands on my hips taking in huge quantities of 'country fresh air' . . . saying things like: And just think . . . it's only a couple of hours from the city.

RICHARD. No.

JULIE. Can I just do nothing?

RICHARD. (*He enters and stands R. of pillar.*) Whatever makes you happy.

JULIE. You make me happy. (RICHARD *crosses to sofa, pulls off sheet and throws it under the sofa. He looks up at her.*) Don't look at me like that?

RICHARD. Like what, Julie?

JULIE. Like you were doing.

RICHARD. But I don't know what I was doing.

JULIE. You were looking at me . . . (RICHARD *crosses to her. He starts off seriously but gets more playful as he goes on.*)

RICHARD. Yes, but I don't know how I was looking at you. For the last couple of months you've accused me of looking at you a certain way . . . So tell me . . . Do I look at you sneaky with half shut eye. No? Brazenly with bulging pupils? No? Does my look make you want to cringe . . . to crawl . . . to cry? Does it begin with a letter "C"? Am I getting warm? Is it bigger than a pine box?

JULIE. Oh forget it. All my problems turn into your

showcases. (*He goes and sits on sofa. Once again his look asks the question. She responds. She sits* u. s. *on sofa.*) I don't know. I just feel so defensive lately. I run into old friends and have to defend myself for having changed . . . I run into recent friends and have to defend myself for not having changed enough. I go to a store to buy lipstick and I just know this checkout girl thinks I've been duped by the latest T.V. commercial and I just want to scream at her: No, dearie, I haven't been duped . . . I've been buying this same lipstick for years.

RICHARD. I feel the same way when I go to Baskin-Robbins and want a dip of peppermint swirl. Right away you're a fag. So I order chocolate, two scoops like a man.

JULIE. And all of a sudden all of my friends have become Hindus or Buddhists or something . . . Maureen asked me just last week . . . Julie, honey, she said . . . are you still a Christian? You'd think she was accusing me of wearing pleated skirts or something.

RICHARD. You shouldn't listen to Maureen.

JULIE. I didn't. I got real upset and started screaming at her.

RICHARD. That should tell her you're still a Christian. All in all it sounds like a good thing we came up here for a while.

JULIE. You're absolutely right. I think the damn city was getting to us . . . It's nice to be alone and cut off from everybody . . . and I'm going to take advantage of it.

RICHARD. And what does that mean?

JULIE. You'll find out. If you think you're crazy about me now . . . you just wait. I'm going to start exercising . . . blossoming right in front of your eyes.

It's time I got my titts back in shape. You should see Maureen's titts. She's got a permanent hardening of the nipples or something. I think mine are beginning to sag.

RICHARD. I read about it in the Wall Street Journal. Julie's titts sagged two points in light trading.

JULIE. Just don't sell me short is all I ask. (*She goes to the bathroom. As soon as she's gone there's a change in* RICHARD. *His physical 'pose' changes. His movements become angular and quick rather than soft and slow. He goes to his briefcase. Opens the snap locks so they don't make noise. Keeps his eye on the bathroom. Reaches inside the briefcase, takes out a gun.* JULIE *is heard uttering a cry from the bathroom. He quickly puts the gun back in the briefcase.* JULIE *rushes out of the bathroom.* RICHARD *returns to his former physical posture.* JULIE *is very upset.*) There was somebody at the window. (RICHARD *heads for the bathroom. Knock on the back door.* RICHARD *stops.* JULIE *seems ready to say something. Stays away from door.*)

RICHARD. It's not who you think it is. They wouldn't knock. (*He opens the back door. Flashlight, shotgun and* ANDREW, *the nightwatchman, appear in that order. Stays in doorway—in darkness.*)

ANDREW. Oh, it's you . . . good evening . . . I didn't know . . .

RICHARD. It's Andrew, honey.

JULIE. (*Her fear now turns to anger for having been afraid of nothing.*) You scared the hell out of me.

ANDREW. Sorry . . . but you should've given me a call to tell me you're coming up . . . I saw a light . . . Could've been anybody . . . Burglars . . . or worse . . .

JULIE. Now what the hell would a burglar be doing in the bathroom?

ANDREW. Just what you were doing, Mrs. . . . We're all human beings. (RICHARD *gestures to him not to point the shotgun toward him and* ANDREW *moves it aside slowly.*)

RICHARD. I imagine you've got to get going on your rounds. We don't want to keep you.

ANDREW. Feels strange making my rounds. Nobody up here.

RICHARD. Fine, then you can go home. (JULIE *crosses and sits on sofa.*)

ANDREW. You know I haven't seen you on those T.V. commercials lately.

RICHARD. That's because I haven't made any lately.

ANDREW. Oh, moved up to bigger stuff.

RICHARD. No.

ANDREW. That can only mean one thing.

RICHARD. And it does.

ANDREW. Sorry to hear that. I hate to see a man on his way down. (*He steps forward into the light.* JULIE *is a little stunned by his appearance.*) I've fallen apart myself haven't I.

JULIE. No.

RICHARD. We were just going to bed.

ANDREW. Sure I have. I was fine and then all of a sudden I started getting rickety and senile . . . Same thing happened to my father. A fine figure of a man . . . Had a laugh like a thunderstorm . . . And then one morning there he was . . . sitting at a breakfast table and drooling on his French toast . . . My mother burst out crying.

RICHARD. (*Louder.*) WE WERE JUST GOING TO BED.

ANDREW. I'M NOT DEAF YOU KNOW. I HEARD YOU THE FIRST TIME. SOMETIMES WHEN I DON'T PICK UP ON SOMETHING THAT'S

BEING SAID IT'S BECAUSE I CHOOSE NOT
TO. (*Stops.*) Whew! I'm just starting my rounds and
it feels funny doing it without my dog. Poor thing was
getting blind. I just shot her a while ago. Maybe you
heard the shot?

RICHARD. We didn't hear it.

ANDREW. It's the dampness here . . . The air's so
thick it sucks up noise like a sponge. You could scream
your head off and nobody'd hear you. I know. Well
. . . I suppose you were just getting ready to go to
bed . . . (*Starts to leave.*) Oh yes . . . A young
couple rented the green cottage across from you. One
of them's a man. And the other one's a woman of some
kind. Both black as night . . .

RICHARD. (*He interrupts and picks up on the word.*)
Good night.

ANDREW. Good night. My nephew's up here with his
girl friend. No telling what those kids are doing in my
room . . . Enjoy yourselves. (ANDREW *leaves.*)

JULIE. I thought you told me last week that you had
called Andrew and told him we're coming.

RICHARD. Well I didn't. I knew he'd want to stop
by and bring up the whole thing again and I just didn't
want him upsetting you.

JULIE. (*Half joke.*) So, ulterior motives after all.
Any others?

RICHARD. Nope.

JULIE. Did you know you only say nope when you're
lying?

RICHARD. Nope.

JULIE. Coming to bed?

RICHARD. Yep . . . I'll just lock up. (*She goes into
the bedroom. As soon as she does* RICHARD *takes the
gun out of the briefcase. He looks for a place to hide*

it . . . he puts it under the sofa. He locks the doors.
Turns out the light. There's a shaft of light coming
from the bedroom . . . He goes inside the bedroom.)

ACT ONE

Scene 2

Morning.

JULIE *opens the refrigerator. Takes out the bag of*
groceries. Looks inside it unhappily. Takes out a
loaf of sliced bread from the bag. Peeks inside
bag again.

JULIE. Is there something you can make with bread
and catsup?

RICHARD. (O. S.) There is but you shouldn't. Let's
skip breakfast.

JULIE. (*She takes out a yogurt for herself and begins*
to eat it.) I had such a stupid dream. I dreamt I was
living in this country where it's punishable by death
to be caught naked. What am I going to do, I kept
saying in this absurd voice, I haven't got a thing to
wear. (*She waits for some kind of a reply from*
RICHARD. *None comes.* RICHARD *comes out. He is wear-*
ing sweatpants . . . sweatshirt . . . sneakers . . . He
has been shaving. He is holding his chin. What follows
has a ring of a 'routine' that RICHARD *and* JULIE *have*
done before. She looks at his chin.) What's the matter?

RICHARD. Cut myself shaving.

JULIE. Well . . . put some toilet paper on it.

RICHARD. I did. (*He lets go the hand and a five foot*

*length of toilet paper falls to the floor attached to the
nick on his chin at the top. He gets the response he
wants from her and then he jauntily swings the toilet
paper over his shoulder like a scarf. Pauses. Takes the
bottom edge of the T.P. and examines it.*) A message
from Iago?

JULIE. I don't like your Iago, my lord. He's such
a little turd.

RICHARD. (*He [Othello] reads the message.*) He
says you have been unfaithful to me, Desdemona.

JULIE. He would say that . . . horny little runt.

RICHARD. Silence! (*He tears off the end of the toilet
paper.*) Is this thy handkerchief, Desdemona?

JULIE. Call me Mona, my lord.

RICHARD. Skipping ahead. Set you down this . . .
(JULIE *becomes a secretary taking down dictation.*)
That in Aleppo once . . .

JULIE. Two P's in Aleppo?

RICHARD. Where a malignant and turbaned Turk
beat a Venetian and traduced the State . . . I took by
the throat (*Takes himself by the throat.*)   the cir-
cumcised dog and smote him thus. (*He smites himself
over the head with it. Falls on the floor.* JULIE *ap-
plauds. He rises.*)

JULIE. You must be feeling good to die so early in
the day.

RICHARD. FIRST TIME I slept so well since the last
time we were up here.

JULIE. Don't you think you should give Myra a
call?

RICHARD. Why?

JULIE. What if something comes up?

RICHARD. Like what?

JULIE. Richard, is there something the matter?

RICHARD. I think Myra and I are slowly parting
company.

JULIE. AFTER all these years. Do you have another agent in mind?

RICHARD. (*He crosses into kitchen and pours himself some water.*) I really don't know . . . It's always the same thing . . . You get any agent and the first thing they do is hype up your future . . . just as Myra did . . . She had all these great hopes and plans for my acting career . . . I was supposed to be a star by now . . . so it's kind of awkward for her to call me up for some two bit voice-over spot . . . Both of us have to pretend that we never had those hopes and plans . . . it's painful . . .

JULIE. You're just too good an actor not to be working . . .

RICHARD. You really think so?

JULIE. Of course I do.

RICHARD. I have a shocking new theory why a lot of actors can't find work. It's not because of some conspiracy of producers and directors . . . It's because they're rotten actors.

JULIE. But you're not one of them.

RICHARD. But, what if I was?

JULIE. But, you're not.

RICHARD. But what if I was?

JULIE. But you're not.

RICHARD. But what if I was?

JULIE. Richard, I don't know what you want me to say.

RICHARD. (*He wants to end the whole thing.*) Ach . . . forget it. I think I'll go out and shoot a few. (*Goes to bedroom.*)

JULIE. You know what . . . I can't remember my mother's telephone number . . . I was going to call her . . .

RICHARD. Oxford something. You always want to call her when we're out of the city.

JULIE. I know. That way she can't ask me to come over.

RICHARD. (*He comes out of closet with basketball.*) I thought you like to visit her.

JULIE. (*He comes back out with sneakers, and stands looking out on basketball court.*) I do . . . but I feel a little guilty because you don't have a mother yourself.

RICHARD. Sometimes I think the only reason you love me is because I'm an orphan.

JULIE. I wonder whatever happened to all those kids you used to tell me about. T-bone and all the rest of them . . . (HENRY *comes out of the house and crosses to basketball court, doing warm-up exercises.*) Don't you orphans have reunions or something? What was that thing T-bone used to say? (*Just then we hear a basketball bouncing outside the house.* RICHARD *goes to the window and looks out.*)

RICHARD. Well sonovabitch.

JULIE. What's the matter?

RICHARD. You won't believe this. Guess who the black guy is who rented the green house. Just guess.

JULIE. (*She comes over and looks out of the window.*) Oh, I've seen him.

RICHARD. You've seen him! He got the last three commercials I was up for. Mr. Residuals we call him. Bastard. Look at him . . . bouncing his black balls across my court.

JULIE. You sure it's him?

RICHARD. I guess I'll go and find out.

JULIE. Oh Jesus . . . You're not going to carry a grudge are you?

RICHARD. I'd prefer a club.

JULIE. I don't need to start worrying about this . . .
I really don't . . .

RICHARD. Nothing to worry about. I can take care
of myself. (*Starts going out.*) Maybe we'll just have
a friendly little game of one on one. My court. His
ball.

JULIE. You're not going to make trouble are you?

RICHARD. Nope. (RICHARD *drops his ball and goes
out. Lights up on the court, fade on the cottage.*)

ACT ONE

SCENE 3

*Basketball court. Although the basketball court is
near both houses we do not see the houses. The
court is a separate area. It feels alien somehow.
Stark. There is only one basket and it's attached
to a steel pole . . . a red steel pole perhaps . . .
and the effect of the basket and the net and the
place in general gives it the look of the gallows.*
HENRY *is dribbling around and shooting. He's
wearing sweatpants . . . sweatshirt . . . sneakers
. . . As most solo players would do he seems to be
pretending he's in a game . . . he fakes around
imaginary opponents . . . drives toward the
basket and around and finally shoots. He does
not see* RICHARD *watching him.*

RICHARD *waits for the moment when* HENRY *has
stopped to shoot. As* HENRY *takes careful aim at
the basket* RICHARD *comes closer to him from
behind and then, just as* HENRY'S *about to release
the ball* RICHARD *lets go with:*

RICHARD. Hi there!

(HENRY *is startled. His shot goes way off the mark. But* HENRY *does not stay startled too long. He recovers . . . both the ball and himself.*)

HENRY. Hi . . . you must be the other people who're up here.

RICHARD. Sounds like you met Andrew already.

HENRY. Oh yeah. Henry Jefferson. (*They shake hands.*)

RICHARD. Richard Hennessy.

HENRY. You look familiar kind of.

RICHARD. You kind of do too.

HENRY. You an actor?

RICHARD. I try to be.

HENRY. Ah . . . it's a rotten business.

RICHARD. For some.

HENRY. I hope you don't mind me using your court.

RICHARD. The court of Richard is honoured to have you, Sir Henry. (RICHARD *crosses* D. R.)

HENRY. You want to shoot a few? (HENRY *passes the ball to* RICHARD. RICHARD *looks at it.*)

RICHARD. Hmm . . . man's got a leather ball. Golly. Played college?

HENRY. St. John's. You?

RICHARD. St. Bonaventure. Starter?

HENRY. No. Sub. You?

RICHARD. Same. Guard?

HENRY. Yeap. Too short for that even.

RICHARD. Same here.

(*There's a feeling here that* HENRY *is waiting for* RICHARD *to do something with the ball. Either shoot it or give it back to* HENRY *. . . There's* *also a feeling here that* RICHARD *is doing it on purpose.* HENRY'*s the kind of man who needs to keep something going. His metabolism does not allow for a pause. If he can't dribble the ball he's got to talk.*)

HENRY. It's a shame, isn't it, what's happening to the Knicks. I mean they were blowing people off the court until that whole default business hit the city . . . and then they just fell apart. It's an interesting connection don't you think . . . the fact that the sport franchises are a barometer of the city's confidence.

RICHARD. (*If* RICHARD *were ready to give up the ball and start playing a little* HENRY'*s speech makes him pause. He is on to something.*) Yes, it's very interesting. So interesting in fact that somebody even took the trouble to write about that very theory in the New York Times. (RICHARD *throws to* HENRY.)

HENRY. I wasn't really pretending that it was mine. (HENRY *throws back.*)

RICHARD. Neither was I. (RICHARD *dribbles up to basket and stops.*) In the same issue, the very same issue in which that theory appeared there was also another interesting story . . . wasn't there?

HENRY. There were a lot of stories.

RICHARD. Sure . . . but all of them weren't interesting. The one I had in mind was.

HENRY. What story was that?

RICHARD. Well, you see, I was wondering if you remembered it.

HENRY. Maybe I didn't read it.

RICHARD. But it was right next to the article about the Knicks . . . You could hardly miss it . . .

HENRY. Maybe if you refreshed my memory.

RICHARD. Now there's a thought. You see . . . they

had a story about this place . . . about those killings
that took place in this place . . . about how nobody
comes here any more and how this and how that and
how among other things they never caught the person
or persons who did it and how that's what's keeping
people away.

HENRY. Oh yeah . . . I think I do remember
now . . .

RICHARD. I bet you do. Well, I just thought it was
interesting that you and I were up here, I guess we're
not afraid.

(A WOMAN *appears in a wheelchair at this point. Her
name is* RACHEL. *She is* HENRY's *wife.* JULIE *also
appears in her cottage putting some books away
and cleaning up.)*

RACHEL. Henry, could you help?

HENRY. Sure . . . Be right back. (*He pushes her
offstage as* RICHARD *watches and then* HENRY *returns.*)
Oh, I'm sorry . . . that's my wife, Rachel.

RICHARD. (*He picks up on it.*) I'm sorry that's my
wife, Julie. Well, Henry . . . you game for a little
game?

HENRY. Little one on one?

RICHARD. Yeah.

HENRY. That might be interesting.

RICHARD. Ten point game . . . winner's ball out
. . . got to win by two.

HENRY. It's your court, Rich.

RICHARD. It's your ball, Henry. (RICHARD *takes off
his sweatshirt. The way he takes it off hints strongly
that he's taking this game seriously. Seeing him take*

it off HENRY *responds in kind . . . and in spirit of the gesture as well. Having taken off his sweatshirt* RICHARD *reveals a T-shirt with a large "ADIDAS" written on it.* HENRY *reveals a T-shirt with a large "PUMA" written on it. Both of them take in these signs on their chests with cool smiles of acknowledgement.* RICHARD *throws the ball to* HENRY *to take out.* HENRY *starts dribbling.*) Here comes Henry, the ball driving man. (HENRY *is dribbling slowly, his back to* RICHARD. RICHARD *guards him closely to say the least . . . Too closely . . . Pesters him . . . Pushes him on his ass with his hand??? And then, suddenly, he reaches around in an obvious foul . . . steals the ball from* HENRY. HENRY *pauses thinking it was a foul. And while he pauses* RICHARD *drives in for an easy layup.*) One zip. Winner's ball out. (RICHARD *takes the ball out.* HENRY's *a little off balance by the whole thing. But he decides to be cool. He starts guarding* RICHARD. *But* RICHARD *doesn't seem to be fond of being guarded. He is backing into* HENRY *the whole way . . . pushing him back . . . and then . . . when* HENRY *finally decides to stand his ground* RICHARD *really slams into him . . . knocks him down to the ground and goes in to score an easy layup.*) Two zip.

HENRY. (*Still on ground.*) I think we've had a few fouls here.

RICHARD. Oh yeah . . . funny . . . I don't see any referees around here.

HENRY. Oh, I get it. (HENRY *fouls* RICHARD *in a flagrant manner and takes ball away from* RICHARD *and shoots.*) Two to one. (*They start to get into place again, as the lights come up on the* HENNESSY *cottage and down on the court.*)

ACT ONE

SCENE 4

HENNESSY *cottage.*

JULIE *is dressed in a pair of tight and rather revealing leotards. She is doing yoga exercises . . . listening to a record of instructions.*

RECORD. *Sit back on your heels as in Figure 23. Extend arms out over the knees stretching out the fingers for maximum separation. Lean your torso forward and rolling the eyeballs upwards in your sockets stick out the tongue till it reaches the tip of your chin. Hold for fifteen seconds.*

(*There is a knock on the door. Louder.* JULIE *stops the record. Goes to the door. Opens it. It's* ANDREW. *He looks at her and is startled. Then he laughs. Then he stops laughing.*)

ANDREW. I thought you were naked. Took my breath away.

JULIE. No it didn't. (*Allusion to his breath is made.*)

ANDREW. Been drinking a little . . . not much at all . . . Not what you call heavy drinking . . . not your drinking drinking . . .

JULIE. What do you want, Andrew?

ANDREW. Oh, yes . . . I was wondering if you'd seen my dog.

JULIE. You're drunk. You said you shot your dog last night.

ANDREW. Shoot her I did. And I was going to bury her today. Couldn't bury her last night. It's frightening burying things at night. I should've shot her and buried her in daytime only I couldn't bear to shoot her in daylight . . . She's got eyes . . . they're blind . . . but they're eyes . . . and blind eyes . . .

JULIE. What are you talking about? I don't know what you're talking about.

ANDREW. My dog. I guess I didn't quite kill her. I guess I just wounded her . . . cause she ain't where she was . . . There was a trail of blood . . . but I lost it . . . that's why I was wondering if you'd seen her cause the trail seemed to be heading toward this area . . . (*At this instant* RICHARD *appears at the back door. Pushes* ANDREW *aside.* RICHARD *is bleeding. His face is covered with blood. He has his head tilted back and is holding his hand to his nose.* HENRY *is following him.* HENRY *looks a little apologetic.*)

RICHARD. I'm alright. Just a little accident. My nose ran into Henry's elbow . . . entirely my nose's fault . . . I'll be fine as soon as I survive. (*He heads toward the bathroom. Goes in.*)

HENRY. (*To* JULIE.) I'm real sorry.

ANDREW. I don't care. It's not my nose.

HENRY. I was speaking to Mrs. Hennessy.

ANDREW. It's not her nose either. Doesn't she look nude.

JULIE. You'd better leave now, Andrew.

ANDREW. Oh, I get the picture. (*Starts to leave. Stops. Fiddles with the lock.*) A child could break this lock. And you should peek through the curtains before you let someone in. Enjoy yourselves. (*Laughs and leaves. His departure makes* JULIE *much more self-conscious about her leotards.* HENRY *doesn't hide the way he looks at her.*)

HENRY. This is some way to meet a neighbour! My name's Henry Jefferson.

JULIE. Yes . . . I mean I recognized you. (RICHARD *appears in the doorway and looks at them. They don't see him.*) You've done some theatre work, haven't you?

HENRY. Just enough to help me break into T.V. commercials. (*He laughs a little.*)

JULIE. I wish Rich had that attitude. This is going to sound very strange . . . but I wonder if you'd tell me who you have for an agent. (RICHARD *picks this moment to interrupt.*)

RICHARD. (*He crosses between them.*) The kid's back! Half time's over . . . full speed ahead.

HENRY. I don't think we better play any more.

RICHARD. My nose is fine . . . what's left of it.

HENRY. But my knees are not.

RICHARD. Then we resume tomorrow . . . I never quit when I'm ahead.

HENRY. Tomorrow it is. (*Starts to leave.*) You folks want to drop by tonight for a drink or something?

RICHARD. Sure. I'd love to.

HENRY. Great. Any time . . . And . . . sorry . . . it really was an accident.

RICHARD Forget it. It's blood under the bridge so to speak. You got me by accident . . . I'll get you by accident. (*He waves to* HENRY. HENRY *leaves. Closes door.*) Accident my ass. Bastard hit me on purpose. I swear . . . if I had a gun I would have shot him . . . shit. It's bleeding again. (*He holds his nose.*) I better lie down. (*He heads for bedroom.* JULIE *follows*).

JULIE. We really don't have to go tonight.

RICHARD. Oh, we'll go, we'll go. (*They both disappear inside the bedroom. Lights fade on the cottage and up on the pier.*)

BLACKOUT

ACT ONE

Scene 5

Dusk. By the pier. Randy *and* Debbie. Debbie *enters first from the boathouse followed by* Randy *who takes a paint brush from her she was hiding. He carries a pail.*

Randy. I can still smell that perfume on you.

Debbie. It's very expensive. And it lasts a long time.

Randy. It smells like you just put it on. You didn't steal it, did you?

Debbie. Of course not. Do I look like a thief? (Debbie *sits on pier.*)

Randy. No, but then those guys don't look like the types to play ball together, either. I hid behind the bushes and watched them play this morning. They stink. Not only that, they don't even know the rules. (Randy *begins to paint rudder and tiller.*)

Debbie. Successful people make their own rules.

Randy. Oh yeah, what's so successful about them?

Debbie. If you lived in New York you'd know. I saw both of them on television.

Randy. I saw Donald Duck on television too.

Debbie. It certainly wouldn't hurt to get to know them better. In New York it's who you know . . . that's how you get the good jobs. (Randy *laughs.*) What's so funny?

Randy. You talking about jobs. When I used to talk about them you made fun of me. I guess I'm making fun of you now.

Debbie. It's easy for you. You're living off your uncle.

RANDY. (*He crosses to boathouse.*) Everybody lives off somebody. Uncle will die.

DEBBIE. And then what'll you do?

RANDY. I'll rent the cottages he bought up. I'll be a landlord. (*Re-enters with rag cleaning his hands.*)

DEBBIE. I thought you said everybody got frightened off.

RANDY. They're starting to trickle back.

DEBBIE. The lake is all scummy. The cottages are run down.

RANDY. I've learned something about resorts, Debbie. People go to them to complain. It makes going back home easier to take. I'll do all right. Had you married me, Deb, you wouldn't be worrying about money now.

DEBBIE. Who says I'm worried?

RANDY. I watch you when you eat. You eat a lot, Debbie. Just because it's free.

DEBBIE. You're a nice host.

RANDY. I told you. I'm not as sweet as I used to be. I used to think that seeing your breasts was a treat of a lifetime.

DEBBIE. You'd still like to see them.

RANDY. Sure. You always want the toys you didn't get enough of as a kid.

DEBBIE. (*She begins to walk* D, S. *on the pier.*) That's a horrible way of putting it.

RANDY. That's just how I felt. I even cried when you left.

DEBBIE. You did not.

RANDY. I tried. And you know what I did last summer. I went to New York. And I saw you, Debbie.

DEBBIE. Saw me where?

RANDY. I called your parents and they told me you weren't doing too well in the city. They said I should visit you. Maybe you told them to say that.

DEBBIE. I did not. You're making it all up.

RANDY. (*He stops painting and walks toward her.*) I got your address from them and I went to see you. There was this little entryway and I saw your little mailbox with your little name on it. I even pushed this little button to buzz you but you weren't at home. So I pushed another little button and whoever it was buzzed back to open the door. And then I pushed another one. And they, too, buzzed back to open the door. The people in your building are dying for visitors, it seems. But I didn't go in. Right outside your building there was this car. The door was open and I sat in the car til' you came home. I saw you walking, Debbie. And you weren't skipping along in that breezy way of yours. No, you were sort of plodding home. And I saw you open your little mailbox . . . I saw it all, Debbie.

DEBBIE. You're making it all up. All of it. I was probably very tired when you saw me. If you saw me.

RANDY. That's all I was saying. That you looked tired.

DEBBIE. No, you weren't. You were saying something else. (*He goes back to painting.*)

RANDY. That's all, Debbie. It was a very hot day. It's cool here. Even in summer. Damp but cool. And you're getting to look like your old self again. Breezy Debbie. All those girls in school tried to imitate the way you walked but none could. Do you want to get married?

DEBBIE. Is that a proposal or something?

RANDY. No. It's a question. I already proposed once and you turned me down. It's your turn now.

DEBBIE. So you can say no and get even.

RANDY. Maybe I won't say "no."

DEBBIE. I didn't come here to make decisions,

Randy. I've been on my own for two years now and it wears you out. Being the one who's responsible for everything. Making decisions for everything. I just want to rest and have things happen like they used to. (*She gets up suddenly and starts to leave.*) I think I'll go back to the city tomorrow.

RANDY. I'll ask you to stay if you want. (*She exits. He picks up bucket and follows her.*)

ACT ONE

SCENE 6

RICHARD *and* JULIE *enter through Jefferson's cottage.* RICHARD *says "goodnight, and thank you."* JULIE *enters their cottage and sits on sofa.* RICHARD *follows and turns on the light.*

RICHARD. That was certainly a lovely little get-together. Made you feel good inside . . . nice and warm . . . like open heart surgery.

JULIE. It's just . . . Goddammit, I was looking forward to a little get-together with another woman. If anything, I was worried you and Henry might go at it . . . instead . . . I still don't know what got into her. It's not funny.

RICHARD. Hell, I thought it was hilarious. The way Rachel looked at us when we came in. Even her hair was frowning. And there you were: a bottle of wine in your hand and a smile on your face: Hi, we're the people next door. So what, Rachel says.

JULIE. I couldn't believe it. I was stunned.

RICHARD. So were we all. Things got so silent you could hear a jaw drop. And then you remember the wine. That should break the ice! How about some cold duck, you say. Rachel loves cold duck, Henry says. I hate cold duck, Rachel says.

JULIE. She's got to be crazy.

RICHARD. Damn right she's crazy. That's why I couldn't understand why you kept trying to ingratiate yourself. Poor Henry. He's stuck with that . . . But you, I mean you really tried. You started making plans with Rachel . . . let's all of us get together in the city . . . for a concert . . . for a show . . . for a movie . . . You were going on like a human ticketron.

JULIE. I know. I know. She just made me feel so nervous . . . like the whole thing was my fault.

RICHARD. "The Cold Duck's getting warm," you finally said. "I don't care if the damn duck dies," Rachel snaps back and tries to get away from you. She shifts her wheelchair into overdrive . . . only your shirt gets caught in the damn thing and she's pulling you along with her and you're trying ever so nicely not to embarrass her and free yourself at the same time. And that somehow summed it up. You just tried too hard, honey, that's all.

JULIE. I know I tried too hard. I've been doing that lately and I don't know why. I'm almost desperate to make friends out of strangers.

RICHARD. It's not quite that bad.

JULIE. Sure it is. Especially when you're around. I so much want to have people like me in front of you.

RICHARD. You don't have to prove anything to me, Julie.

JULIE. It's not to prove . . . it's just that . . . you know . . . we all think we have some hidden marvelous side to us . . . and if only the atmosphere were right everybody would see it.

RICHARD. I see enough.

JULIE. But I think there's more to me than you see.

RICHARD. The real Julie Hennessy! Who is she? Does anyone really know?

JULIE. I'm serious, dammit.

RICHARD. We didn't come up here to be serious, dammit.

JULIE. Well, maybe I did.

RICHARD. So-o you're the one with ulterior motives.

JULIE. I just feel a need to change. I don't know where I fit in today. I remember watching my mother when I was small. Her whole day seemed orchestrated like a fancy waltz and she just danced her way through the day. She knew what was expected of her. She had a framework.

RICHARD. But that world is gone, Julie.

JULIE. That's what everyone keeps saying. It's all gone and we're all so goddamn free to flounder about. I just wish there was something. This will sound silly but if nothing else I wish I believed in sin.

RICHARD. In the orphanage where I grew up this Sister Regina talked about sins all the time. We didn't get along. I kept snickering and making cracks and she kept threatening to curse me for being a heathen. Oh, my head was full of these wonderful Cecil B. DeMille images of what it would be like to be cursed . . . and I kept going after her until finally the poor woman lost all control and jumped to her feet, and mustering all the majesty the moment allowed, she thundered at me: I CURSE YOU! I stood there trembling . . . waiting for the roof and the sky to open up and for God to appear to finish the job . . . but . . . nothing happened. I started crying. The other kids in the room thought it was because I was afraid. It was disappointment. We became good friends. We shared a secret. There was no God. No sin.

JULIE. If there's no God, my mother used to say, then we're all devils.

RICHARD. For once I think your mother is right.

(*A noise makes both of them pause. It's a strange, soft noise . . . a soft whining and then added to it something like scratching on the back door. It is not a sound to make one start or scream . . . but it is the type of noise in the night that the more you listen to it the more uncomfortable it seems.* RICHARD *walks slowly toward the door . . . he gestures* JULIE *to stay back, but she follows him. He opens the door. And then he turns the porch light on and as he does,* JULIE *screams.*)

JULIE. What's that? (*Crosses to* U. S. *and looks out.*) It must be Andrew's dog.

RICHARD. I thought he said he killed it. God . . . it's bleeding all over the place.

JULIE. It's coming in. Don't let it come in, Rich. Oh, it's crying . . . I can't bear it. Do something, Rich.

RICHARD. Do what?

JULIE. Do something. I can't bear it. (*She starts screaming . . . crying.*)

RICHARD. Stop screaming. Stop it. Do you hear me. Stop it.

JULIE. It's stomach is all coming out. Finish it off or something. Finish it off, Richard. I can't bear it. (*She continues screaming as if to cover up any sound the wounded animal might be making.*)

RICHARD. I can't think when you do that. I can't think, damn you. I can't think. Shut up! Shut up!

JULIE. You're just standing there! You're just standing there, Richard. (RICHARD *cannot tolerate her screaming. He reaches suddenly for the gun in its hiding place. Pulls it out and without pausing, he steps outside and fires into the dog. It's all very sudden and fast. He shuts the door.)* Is she dead?

RICHARD. Yes.

JULIE. I just couldn't bear to see her suffer like that. Oh, God, she probably came here to hide from Andrew.

RICHARD. Stop saying "she." It's a dog. *(There is a knock on the door and then the door opens. It's* HENRY. *He looks at the dead dog in the doorway and then at the gun in* RICHARD's *hand.)*

HENRY. Sorry to burst in like this . . . but I heard the shots. Is everything all right?

RICHARD. Yeah, everything's fine.

HENRY. *(To* JULIE.) Some evening, eh? Well . . . good night then.

RICHARD. Good night, Henry. (HENRY *leaves.* RICHARD *feels awkward with the gun in his hand. Doesn't know where to put it. Sticks it into his jacket pocket.)*

JULIE. You never told me you had a gun.

RICHARD. The subject never came up.

JULIE. What other subjects never came up?

RICHARD. Please, Honey. I'm very upset. You seemed so damned afraid of coming up here that some of your fear rubbed off on me. So I bought this stupid thing for protection. I didn't want to tell you. I never thought there would be a reason. I've never killed anything before. *(He sits down, looking shaken by what he has done.* JULIE *comes up to him.)*

JULIE. I'm sorry. I lost my head screaming like that. Let's go to bed.

RICHARD. In a second. I just want to calm down a bit. *(She leaves for the bedroom. As soon as she does there is a change in* RICHARD. *He takes the gun from his pocket and looks at it. He stands up. He throws the gun in the air and catches it. Then he pauses. Sees a bright yellow towel draped over the chair. Picks up the towel and wraps the gun into it. And then he pulls off the towel revealing the gun as if he were surprising somebody. LIGHTS DIM AROUND HIM.*)

ACT ONE

SCENE 7

Basketball court.

HENRY *and* DEBBIE. HENRY *has the ball in his hands.*

HENRY. It all depends. If the commercial runs a long time then I get a lot of residuals. If it doesn't it's just the small flat fee.

DEBBIE. I know a girl in the city. And her sister's a production assistant.

HENRY. Yes?

DEBBIE. Is it hard to get a job like that?

HENRY. It all depends on who you know.

DEBBIE. That's just it. I don't know many people.

HENRY. All it takes is one or two.

DEBBIE. I know one or two . . . but they're not the ones. (RICHARD *comes toward them, carrying a rolled-up yellow towel.* HENRY *passes him the ball.*)

HENRY. Rich, Debbie here would like to be a production assistant.

RICHARD. That's a good start. Remember that girl, Michele something?

HENRY. Oh, right. We got her a job as a production assistant.

RICHARD. And she went on to bigger and better things. And she wasn't half as pretty as Debbie here.

HENRY. That's right. (RANDY *appears at the* U. R.)

RANDY. Debbie. Want to go on that walk now?

DEBBIE. Oh, all right. See you guys later. (*She exits with* RANDY.)

HENRY. (*Smiles.*) Guy . . . I haven't been called a guy in years.

RICHARD. My wife used to wear the same perfume she had on. (*For a moment he seems lost in the memory and then, quite consciously he pulls himself out of it. He dribbles the ball. He drives for the basket and then suddenly passes it to* HENRY.) West to Baylor. (HENRY *dribbles and passes it back to* RICHARD.)

HENRY. Baylor to West.

RICHARD. Mr. Clutch with the touch. (RICHARD *dribbles. Stops a la West . . . jumps . . . passes it suddenly to* HENRY *who whips it behind his back and back to* RICHARD, *who in turn does the same thing and back to* HENRY. *A frenzy of passing artistry ensues . . . or at least attempted artistry . . .* HENRY, *keeping up the chatter: "Feed me . . . feed me . . . over here . . . feed me . . . " The passing continues until a crescendo is reached and both of them are exhausted, ending up with either of them actually shooting the ball and missing.*)

HENRY. Man, if we could only shoot the way we can pass . . .

RICHARD. We wouldn't be playing the passing game.

HENRY. Sometimes when nobody's around . . . I can hit from anywhere.

RICHARD. No shit. And sometimes when nobody's around I can do King Lear playing all the parts and at the same time being a critic in the audience writing a rave review of my performances AND . . . through a time warp watching all the people I hate reading the raves I got.

HENRY. Oh, man, you're good. Good and warped.

RICHARD. Yes, I am, Henry. (*Something about the way he says this makes* HENRY *want to get back to basketball. He takes the ball.*)

HENRY. I had one ambition when I was a kid.

RICHARD. And I bet it wasn't to grow up to be the best husband there is.

HENRY. It had to do with basketball.

RICHARD. Oh yeh, let me guess . . . Oh, there is such a look in your eye, Sir Henry, as if to hint the ashes of a dream lie there. Was it some lofty goal? To fly perhaps? To soar . . . and then to slam dunk that ball! Woosh!

HENRY. You got it. The ol' stuff shot! (RICHARD *makes a hoop from his arms and* HENRY *dribbles a few times and then "slam dunks" the ball in the "hoop." As soon as this is done they reverse their roles and* RICHARD *does the stuff shot into* HENRY'S *arms. Perhaps they have another round . . . perhaps not . . . The crucial element is that* HENRY *is interested in keeping it going but* RICHARD *stops suddenly. Fakes* HENRY *out. Just as he's about to dunk the ball into the hoop* RICHARD *made out of his arms,* RICHARD *pulls his arms aside and stops.*)

RICHARD. I'm thinking, Henry. And you know what I'm thinking. I'm thinking if there's a will, Henry, there's a way, and if there's a way to fulfill our secret ambitions, it must be pursued. (HENRY *is holding the ball.* RICHARD *picks up the rolled-up towel. Wipes forehead with it and then lets it unroll, but holds on to it.*)

HENRY. What are you getting at, Rich?

RICHARD. I know how we can dunk the ball. (HENRY *laughs.*)

HENRY. Sure. Lower the rim. (*His reply was meant to be a joke but he realizes that his joke is* RICHARD's *plan. His laugh changes and turns into a comment on such a plan.*) You're kidding. Oh, wow. You got to be kidding. C'mon, we're not that hard up.

RICHARD. Sure we are. Besides, who says it's got to be at that height anyway. Did God put it there? Did we vote on it? Is it a natural phenomenon?

HENRY. No, but . . .

RICHARD. But what?

HENRY. It's real world. You don't mess with that. I mean, what's the point of having standards if you . . .

RICHARD. (*Interrupts.*) We can set our own standards.

HENRY. No.

RICHARD. C'mon. Let's do it.

HENRY. I said "no." (RICHARD *drops the towel, presses the "gun" into* HENRY's *stomach. We do not see the gun.* HENRY's *back obscures it.* HENRY *reacts to it.*)

RICHARD. Now we're going to do as I say or I'll shoot, damnit.

HENRY. Take it easy, man. Take it easy. Put that thing away.

RICHARD. Standards. You've got a lot of goddamn nerve to use that word after all the ass kissing you've been doing. Tell me. How did you get all those jobs? It sure as hell isn't because of your talent now, is it? You've made life rough for me, you know that.

HENRY. I don't know what you're talking about, man!

RICHARD. Don't give me that "man" stuff. I told you I'd get even. You got me "by accident." Well, now I'm going to get you by accident.

HENRY. Don't do it.

RICHARD. Goodbye, Henry. (RICHARD *shoots.* HENRY *falls. Only now do we realize that* RICHARD *had a transistor radio in his hand. The "blast" of music was the bullet. Both of them are amused by the play.* HENRY *gets up laughing.*)

HENRY. Now why would you want to play a silly game like that?

RICHARD. To see if you'd play along. Now, c'mon. How about the rim? (HENRY *smiles.*)

HENRY. You're rushing me. Maybe tomorrow. I'd like to sleep on it.

RICHARD. Fair enough. Good night.

HENRY. See you in the morning. (*Neither of them leave.*)

RICHARD. (*Yawning.*) 'Morning, Henry. Sleep well?

HENRY. Yes. Fine. (*The words "Yes, Fine," are the go-ahead for the lowering of the rim.* RICHARD *picks up on it instantly.*)

RICHARD. Won't take a second. (HENRY *holds the ball.* RICHARD *gets a bench, climbs up and begins to loosen the rim.* HENRY *is trying to shake some nerves out of himself. Loosen up.*)

HENRY. I can't understand it. I'm getting goosebumps just thinking about it.

RICHARD. Don't worry. Nobody's looking. There's no witnesses.

HENRY. What about you?

RICHARD. I'm a co-conspirator. (*The rim is lowered.* HENRY *is still hesitant.*)

HENRY. Amazing. It feels like we're changing the Constitution or something.

RICHARD. C'mon. Over the rim.

HENRY. Hell with it. Over the rim it is. Feed me. (*He throws the ball to* RICHARD. RICHARD *passes it back to him.* HENRY *catches it on the run. He drives. He cries out loudly as he stuffs the ball down the hole.*)

BLACKOUT

END OF ACT ONE

ACT TWO

Scene 1

The pier by the lake.

JULIE *is sitting on the pier. Her jeans are rolled up above her knees and she's applying suntan lotion to them.* ANDREW *pushes* RACHEL *in her wheelchair onto the pier. He's got his shotgun slung over his shoulder.* JULIE *turns to look at* RACHEL *and then she turns away.*

RACHEL. Sorry. I didn't mean to intrude.

JULIE. It's common property.

ANDREW. Like hell it is. It's my property. I suppose you women want to sunbathe in the nude. Don't mind me if you see me looking at you from afar. I can't see from far but I do enjoy the thought that I'm missing something. Guess I'll go fishing.

JULIE. With a shotgun.

ANDREW. Yes m'am, this is a foul lake. Any fish that could survive in this lake I wouldn't want to take out alive. Enjoy yourselves. (*He leaves.*)

RACHEL. Isn't that them on the other side?

JULIE. Who?

RACHEL. Richard and Henry. (RACHEL *points.* JULIE *looks.*)

JULIE. Yes, I think it is.

RACHEL. Did you come down to keep an eye on them?

JULIE. No, I didn't even know they were there til' you . . .

RACHEL. (*Interrupts.*) Look at them. Walking along the shore like a couple of lovers. There they go. Push-

40

ing each other in the water. Rambunctious rascals.
Certainly strikes me as odd.

JULIE. What's that?

RACHEL. How quickly they became inseparable.

JULIE. I guess men have an easier time making
friends.

RACHEL. I bet they're talking about us.

JULIE. We're talking about them.

RACHEL. We're just beginning. They've been at it
for a while.

JULIE. I'm sorry but I find it difficult to . . . to
chat with you after last night. It seems like one of us
should apologize.

RACHEL. It won't be me. You came at a very bad
time and I was glad to see you go. God, you danced
in there with your cold duck like it was a sorority rush.
Oh, it's so nice to have a neighbor. Oh, what a lovely
cabin. Oh, we really must get together.

JULIE. I was just trying to be friendly.

RACHEL. The thing is, everybody is trying it all of
a sudden. Henry's being friendly as hell. Usually we
just sit in silence and all of a sudden . . . well . . .
it's like he's trying to entertain me. Diversions.

JULIE. People change.

RACHEL. So do warts and moles.

JULIE. That's a cruel thing to say.

RACHEL. Would you rather we talked about concerts
and shows and decorating hints.

JULIE. I didn't prepare an agenda. And I don't like
being lectured to by . . . somebody like you.

RACHEL. You mean a cripple?

JULIE. You know damn well that's not what I
meant.

RACHEL. But it does make it easier to dismiss what
I say. If she's so damn smart why can't she walk?

JULIE. How the hell did you become like that?

RACHEL. You mean a cripple?

JULIE. I mean nothing of the sort. (*Almost without realizing it,* JULIE *is rolling down her jeans.*)

RACHEL. Oh, don't hide your legs on my account. No pity, please.

JULIE. And why not? What is wrong with pity?

RACHEL. I don't need it. It's diverting.

JULIE. It's a fine human feeling.

RACHEL. This is no time to be human.

JULIE. I've heard that before.

RACHEL. Did you know that people were killed up here?

JULIE. Of course, I knew.

RACHEL. Aren't you frightened?

JULIE. Yes, a little.

RACHEL. And still you came?

JULIE. I am here.

RACHEL. And whose idea was it to come here? Yours or Richard's?

JULIE. Mine.

RACHEL. In my case it was Henry's.

JULIE. That's your affair.

RACHEL. No, it's Henry's affair.

JULIE. Then take it up with him.

RACHEL. Since he's taking it up with Richard I thought I'd take it up with you.

JULIE. (*She crosses to* RACHEL.) Look . . . you seem to have something on your mind and I'm tired of trying to guess what it is.

RACHEL. If you want I'll tell you. Henry tried to kill me.

JULIE. I suppose you expect me to believe that.

RACHEL. I wasn't always like this.

JULIE. No, of course not. Your husband made you the way you are.

RACHEL. That's right. And now he doesn't like to be reminded of it.

JULIE. Every woman I've met lately has worked out some elaborate excuse for being the way she is. To hear them talk they were all once warm and giving people and then something happened. And it's never their fault. No. It's not that they're now cold and dead and hostile, not at all, it's just a reaction to their environment. Believe me, your excuse, as preposterous as it sounds, is no worse than the others I've heard. The thing is I'm tired of excuses. I'm tired of trying to deal with them. I'm tired of women trying to initiate me into a world I want no part of.

RACHEL. That still doesn't alter the fact that what I said was true. Henry tried to kill me.

JULIE. (*Crosses center.*) You're a liar. Everything you say is a lie. (*She stands up.*)

RACHEL. But why should it upset you that a strange woman you've chanced to meet and never have to see again unless you want to is a liar? Now whose idea was it really to come up here yours or Richard? (JULIE *begins to walk toward the house as the lights fade to just the rim.*)

ACT TWO

SCENE 2

HENNESSY *cottage. Evening.*

JULIE *and* RICHARD *are sitting down at the table, eating dinner.*

JULIE. (*She crosses to table with coffeepot.*) How's the sandwich?

RICHARD. Delicious.

JULIE. (*Crosses back to kitchen.*) My mother's ultimate description of a bad marriage is when you have cold sandwiches for dinner.

RICHARD. Thank God they're cold. Hot sardine sandwiches . . . Mmmm. (*He smiles.*)

JULIE. (*Sits at table.*) When we get back to the city I'm going to take some cooking lessons.

RICHARD. I thought you took some already and didn't like the whole thing.

JULIE. That was the overnight school of cooking. Everything had to be left overnight to do something. Try having a good night's sleep if you're worrying that your meat is not marinating. (*Pause.*) They have schools and lessons for everything now. Seminars for sex. For religion. For married women. For single women. For divorced women. Different age groups. How to relax. How to intimidate. I saw a test you can take to see if you have a true orgasm or a false one. And a book that tells you how to have multiple orgasms. They're the thing to have. What would we all do if we didn't have problems?

RICHARD. I suppose we'd invent some.

JULIE. Poor world.

RICHARD. It's all right.

JULIE. Wouldn't trade it for anything.

RICHARD. What else did Rachel have to say?

JULIE. About what?

RICHARD. I don't know. I saw you two on the pier for quite some time.

JULIE. And we saw you two by the lake.

RICHARD. Henry and I just talked shop.

JULIE. So did Rachel and I. Shop in our case means husbands.

RICHARD. I guess I'm just surprised that after what she said you still stayed there and listened to her.

JULIE. She saved that for the last.

RICHARD. The woman sounds unhinged. Henry tried to kill her?

JULIE. That's what she said.

RICHARD. I think you should stay away from her. Either she's nuts or she's just toying with you.

JULIE. What does Henry have to say about her?

RICHARD. Subject never came up. (RICHARD *crosses to kitchen; gets juice*.)

JULIE. You just talk shop all this time.

RICHARD. What else?

JULIE. I thought you hated to talk shop.

RICHARD. I guess I've changed.

JULIE. That's what I told Rachel. People change. She thinks you two are seeing an awful lot of each other.

RICHARD. She's just jealous. (*Pours juice in glass and returns it to refrigerator*.)

JULIE. So am I. The way you make friends. I wish I could do it.

RICHARD. It's just that Henry's got a lot of contacts. He's working all the time. I've got to get something going. I feel I owe it to you. (*He sits back down*.)

JULIE. That's a strange thing to say.

RICHARD. You had such high hopes for my career.

JULIE. I thought I was just sharing yours.

RICHARD. When I met you I had none.

JULIE. That's not what you said when we met.

RICHARD. That's not what you wanted to hear.

JULIE. Why does it all keep coming back to me?

RICHARD. Because you made me think I could be better than I was.

JULIE. All I did was love you.

RICHARD. Right. And your kind of love has a way of making a man want to be better.

JULIE. That was never my intent.

RICHARD. But the effect is the same. And I'm grateful.

JULIE. I don't want you to feel grateful.

RICHARD. Why not?

JULIE. Because I don't want it. It has nothing to do with me. It's like you're making me into some other person.

RICHARD. You made me into another person. And I am grateful. Your standards are higher. And I need that.

JULIE. Standards of what?

RICHARD. Of success. Of my potential. I would love to be able to live up to that image you had of me.

JULIE. All I've ever done is support your hopes in good faith. I know you don't intend to but lately you've been putting me in a strange position where my support seems to have become a burden to you.

RICHARD. How could such a thing be possible?

JULIE. I don't know. It's just a feeling. It's stupid, isn't it?

RICHARD. Very. I think talking to Rachel has upset you. (*He clears his plate to the sink.*)

JULIE. I think you're right. Can we sleep on the sofa tonight?

RICHARD. Sure.

JULIE. I haven't been sleeping too well. Maybe if we sleep in an unofficial place . . . like in our first apartment. We used to fall asleep on the sofa all the time . . .

RICHARD. And you used to wear that perfume. The one you wore when we met. I miss it. (*He exits to bedroom.*)

JULIE. For some reason it made me uncomfortable a few months ago. Maybe I felt it was time for a change. (RICHARD *is getting ready to go out. He's putting on his basketball outfit.*) You and Henry going out again? (*He is getting ready, ties his shoes, etc.*)

RICHARD. Yeah, we thought we'd have a game under the lights. See what it's like.

JULIE. I guess we've said everything.

RICHARD. What do you mean?

JULIE. I mean what do you say when you've said everything?

RICHARD. I don't understand.

JULIE. I keep having this insane notion. We've had dinner. We've cleared the dishes. Brushed our teeth . . . put the cap back on the tube and we're ready to say something, only there is nothing left to say. And I don't mean nothing meaningful or crap like that . . . I mean nothing.

RICHARD. And then what?

JULIE. And then we do something terrible just so we can talk about it.

RICHARD. Like what?

JULIE. Oh, all kinds of things. I'll cut my finger with a knife . . . so we can talk about it. And as soon as it's healed I'll whack away at my arm so we can chat about that.

RICHARD. I think that does it. I'm going to take you back to the city.

JULIE. When?

RICHARD. Soon.

JULIE. I'd like that, Rich. Why can't we leave tomorrow? (HENRY *enters. He's ready to play ball.*)

HENRY. What's keeping you? You want to forfeit the game or what?

RICHARD. I was just coming out. (HENRY *bounce-passes the ball to* RICHARD *across the cabin floor.* RICHARD *catches it. To* JULIE.) We won't be long. (RICHARD *dribbles the ball across the cabin.* HENRY *half-guards him.* RICHARD *dribbles around him and out of the cabin.* HENRY *follows.* JULIE *looks after them. They freeze on the court.*)

ACT TWO

SCENE 3

Basketball court. Night. Lights are on in the court.

It's a somewhat chilly evening and the chill is reflected in the dress and physical behavior of HENRY *and* RICHARD. HENRY *tends to shudder more.*

A game of some kind is in progress. Either of them could be dribbling while the other guards. There is a difference in the way they move. It's as if they had been liberated slightly from "classic" basketball moves and are improvising their own. There is something strange about their new moves . . . something frightening. A stranger happening to come upon them would think twice about asking to join the game. One of them shoots. Hit or miss, it doesn't matter, the following dialogue applies.

HENRY. Hold it. Hold it. I'm lost. What the hell's the score?

RICHARD. Let's see . . . it's nine and a half to seven and three quarters.

HENRY. I think we'd better go over the new scoring system again.

RICHARD. Stuff shot—two points. Regular—one point. Hit the backboard—-half point. Hit the rim—three-quarter points. Total miss . . . air ball . . . one quarter.

HENRY. Did you just add that last part?

RICHARD. Sure.

HENRY. No such thing as a miss?

RICHARD. Who needs it? It's our game. (HENRY *bounces the ball a couple of times. Squeezes it.*)

HENRY. Ball's getting soft.

RICHARD. It's the cold air. Makes the molecules contract.

HENRY. (*Laughs.*) Molecules! You believe in molecules . . . atoms .ʾ. . all that stuff?

RICHARD. Not really.

HENRY. I don't either . . . Then how come we go along with it . . . ?

RICHARD. Because there are experts who tell us what exists and what doesn't . . . What's what . . . and what's not. Some jerk comes and reads my meter and sends me a bill and I pay. It's called social trust, Henry.

HENRY. Tell me, Rich. You think you're any good? As an actor? I mean, do you know for sure you're good?

RICHARD. I've been told I am.

HENRY. I've been told I am too.

RICHARD. Got set up to think you were great, eh?

HENRY. Got set up alright.

RICHARD. And you never thought you'd be hustling around for commercials and voice-overs, I bet. It must hurt . . . the comedown.

HENRY. No, you know what hurts? The set-up. The build-up. I never asked for it in the first place. I could have been happy doing what I'm doing . . . I could be happy now.

RICHARD. If there weren't any witnesses of your former glory to remind you that you fell for it.

HENRY. Come on. Let's play. (*He stuffs the ball.*)

RICHARD. So . . . if your past is a crime and you have witnesses to the crime . . . what do you do? You try to get rid of the witnesses. Hmmm. Is that why you tried to kill Rachel?

HENRY. How do you know?

RICHARD. Intuition.

HENRY. Intuition, my ass. Rachel must have said something to Julie. She tells people every now and then, knowing it will get back to me. Just to keep me on my toes. (HENRY *passes the ball to* RICHARD. *They look at each other.*) I was doing a new play and I was lost from the word go. Didn't know what I was doing, so I asked Rachel to come to the rehearsals.

(JULIE *begins to wheel* RACHEL *out onto the pier. The men are not aware of women and vice versa.*)

RACHEL. He wanted something from me. He'd never let me come to rehearsals before—hardly asked me to come. He seemed lost . . . in need of help.

HENRY. I wanted her to tell me the truth . . . that I was making a fool of myself, but no . . . she tells me I'm doing fine.

RACHEL. You're doing fine, I told him. It was a lie but to tell the truth seemed stupid. The man was drowning. So I threw him a life preserver. Something to hold onto. You're doing fine, Henry . . .

HENRY. You're doing fine, Henry. No, she tells me

it's the best she's ever seen me. I start doubting my own lack of talent. Hell, maybe I am good. The play opens and the reviews are terrible. The writer's a moron. The director's worse than the writer. The cast sucks. All except me. They love me. Not only love me but get this . . . they "understood" what I was trying to do. Said stuff like how I reached back . . . way back to some primitive dormant force . . . Yeah . . . and I started falling for it. Maybe, I think, maybe I'm one of those instinctive geniuses . . . one of those "primitives" who doesn't know diddly shit but instinctively makes the right choices . . . Rachel comes to every performance and afterwards feeds me all kinds of goodies . . . Like how she's proud of me . . . In awe of my talent . . .

RACHEL. And he was good. He was great. But he didn't trust it because it wasn't all his . . . Because he was helped and might have to be helped again . . .

HENRY. In awe of my talent! Can you believe that. Over and over again she feeds me that stuff . . . night after night until one evening it hit me. The woman's teasing my ass. I could see it in her eyes . . . she had me. I had fallen for the bait and now she had me. And the more I squirmed . . . the more uncomfortable I felt, the more she poured on the hype and the praise . . .

RACHEL. The more he began to doubt himself the more I tried to reassure him. But that's the last thing he wanted to hear. And yet I couldn't stop. I couldn't. He was like an investment. My little lies had helped create him and damn it all . . . I wasn't lying anymore. I couldn't stop.

HENRY. Inflating me with praise . . . slitting me open and stuffing me full of it . . . telling me what's going to happen to my career . . . star by thirty-five

. . . stuff like that. Finally, late one night I couldn't take it any more. I ran out of the house and went down to the garage just to sit in the car and hear the engine run . . .

RACHEL. It was a habit of his. He'd get in the car . . . turn on the engine and pretend he was zooming along on the turnpikes . . . Back to Chicago to visit his old buddies . . . But for once I wouldn't let him . . . we had to resolve it . . . I went after him . . .

HENRY. But she wouldn't let me alone even there . . . No . . . she snuck down there after me . . . and I saw her coming toward me . . . In the rear-view mirror I saw her.

RACHEL. He saw me. And as soon as he did he shifted that car in reverse. The back-up lights flashed on.

HENRY. She seemed to be standing right in my way . . . I floored it like a primitive sonovabitch I was supposed to be.

RACHEL. It all happened in a split second or so . . . the lights . . . the noise of the engine . . . but in that split second I grew so weary . . . the whole game we were playing . . . the thought of going upstairs again . . . waiting for him . . . wondering what we would say to each other . . . it was too much . . . The car was coming toward me . . . It was going to rush past me but I felt so weary . . . and those lights somehow sucked me forward . . . a half step forward . . . no, not so much a step as collapse . . . The car hit me.

HENRY. The car hit her. Unfortunately, she lived to tell about it. She told everybody . . . the cop people . . . the hospital people . . . the insurance people . . . told them all it was an accident. I felt kind of slimy smug about the whole thing. You know . . . Got the bitch and got away with it . . .

RACHEL. It really was an accident but in the days that followed I could tell that he didn't want to look upon it as an accident. Do you understand? He wanted to think that it was all his doing. That for that split second in the darkness he had been totally in charge. He wanted to think that he had tried to kill me, and for his sake, yes, for his sake, I went along with it.

HENRY. But in the weeks that followed, bit by bit, look by look, it became very clear to me that she knew it was no accident. That she had once again fed me the bait and once again I swallowed it. She had tricked me into another lie and she once again had the upper hand. She loved it. She's got me where she wants me. She made grass out of my ass and now she just rolls across it in her chair.

RICHARD. And then, let me guess, and then you read that interesting story in the Times about all those killings taking place up here and you thought: Hell, why don't I just take Rachel up there, and maybe the killer will be nice enough to take care of her for me. (*He laughs.* HENRY *laughs too.*)

HENRY. It sounds silly as hell but that's exactly why I came.

RICHARD. I know. I know.

HENRY. You too.

RICHARD. Me too.

HENRY. Don't you think they know?

RACHEL. Of course I know what he has in mind and yet . . . I could have refused to come. You could have too. Nobody really forced us to come here and yet there is something that makes me want to see this thing concluded . . . resolved. And there is something else, too. I enjoy the sensation. It makes me a power to be reckoned with. It makes my life seem of greater consequence if it warrants somebody wanting to end it.

It's like being wanted, in a way. (RACHEL *turns and exits. JULIE stands a moment then follows. RICHARD and* HENRY *exit.*)

ACT TWO

SCENE 4

The pier. Day.

DEBBIE *is wearing a bikini. She is putting suntan lotion on her body. She undoes her top and lies down.*

RICHARD *and* HENRY *appear. They seem to have just returned from a stroll around the lake. They see* DEBBIE *and pause. She does not see or hear them.* RICHARD *and* HENRY *exchange looks. Both of them approach* DEBBIE *slowly. On tiptoes almost. They split up. One goes on one side of her. One on the other. They sit down next to her and for a second just watch her.*

RICHARD. Anybody home? (DEBBIE *is startled. Sits up. Her top is ready to fall. She holds it up.*)

DEBBIE. Oh, it's you. Hi.

HENRY. Hi.

RICHARD. Hi. What's that book you're reading?

DEBBIE. Book? I'm not . . .

RICHARD. Just a joke. That's a line guys usually use with girls on the beach.

DEBBIE. Oh, yeah.

RICHARD. Where's your boy friend?

DEBBIE. You mean Randy? Oh, he's not my boy friend. He's just a boy who's a friend. (*She has* HENRY *tie her top for her.*)

HENRY. You see, Rich. I told you there was nothing between her and Randy.

DEBBIE. God, I should hope not.

RICHARD. Actually, that's what we were hoping, too.

DEBBIE. Nothing at all. Zero. I mean . . . if I can't do better than him.

HENRY. I told you, didn't I? Debbie's not your average girl. I've got an eye for such things.

RICHARD. He does. He really does. He's discovered more people. If Henry says somebody has talent . . . he's seldom wrong.

DEBBIE. Talent. I hardly think I have any talent. I mean, maybe I do. I mean, you never know.

HENRY. That's just it. You never do. But somebody else might. (HENRY *takes some lotion from her skin and puts it on his.*)

DEBBIE. I know I could be a production assistant. It's just a feeling . . .

RICHARD. Like the feeling you had when you left for the city. A feeling that you have that "something."

DEBBIE. Yes, exactly. Only . . . you know . . . in the city . . . you forget what it is. I mean, it's easy to forget.

RICHARD. Tell me about it. I remember my early years. It's hard as hell to make it in the city on your own. You start worrying about everything.

DEBBIE. I'll say you do. I mean . . . it's amazing. The kind of things a person worries about. (*She laughs.*) This is so silly but like I worry about what if I lose my job and can't find another one. You know. Will I starve to death or what. (*She laughs.*) Nobody starves to death but still. Or what if nobody ever calls me. You know. There's got to be somebody who never gets a call. What if it's me. Real silly. (HENRY *lies down.*)

RICHARD. You shouldn't have to worry about stuff like that.

DEBBIE. Oh, I know. I mean, I read somewhere that it's just a phase everybody goes through. That made me feel better. (*Laughs.*) But then I started worrying about how long the phase will last. I mean, what if it's some new phase that lasts forever.

RICHARD. That's a real nice perfume you're wearing.

DEBBIE. Oh, thank you. It's just something . . .

RICHARD. The girl I loved used to wear it all the time.

DEBBIE. It's just something . . .

RICHARD. Then she changed and stopped wearing it.

DEBBIE. Maybe she got tired of it.

HENRY. You see what I mean about her voice, Rich?

RICHARD. I think you're right again, Henry. Henry thinks you have a very unusual voice.

DEBBIE. Oh, really. I don't know. I mean, I just open my mouth and there it is.

RICHARD. There are people who would pay a lot of money to use a voice like that.

DEBBIE. To say what?

RICHARD. (*Laughs.*) That you prefer one perfume to another. Commercials, you know. Voice-overs.

DEBBIE. I didn't know they bought voices.

RICHARD. They buy everything, don't they, Henry?

HENRY. They sure do. (HENRY *takes her hands, stands her up.*) They buy hands . . . legs . . . they buy hair and lips . . . sometimes they buy a whole person and give him another voice and sometimes they let him keep his voice . . .

RICHARD. You have lovely hair. (RICHARD *takes her barrette out. He fingers her hairs.*) Shampoos. Hair conditioners. Hair dryers. Curlers and rollers and tints and frosts.

HENRY. And your hands. (*He picks them up and examines them.*) You have beautiful long fingers. Firm nails. Smooth skin. Hand lotions. Nail polishes.

RICHARD. And all you have to do is get one foot in . . . you have the kind of legs they want. Long and lean. For stockings and hose. Bath oils. Depilatories. Sandals and things. And all you have to do is get one little foot in and it's another world.

DEBBIE. (RANDY *enters* D. S. *on pier.*) The thing is . . . I mean . . . I wouldn't know what to do. (HENRY *takes her down to her knees and leans her back.*)

HENRY. It's an instinct. It's not something you know. It's something you have. You just reach back for it.

RICHARD. Potential, that's all you need. Plus somebody to have faith in you. To support you. To remind you that you're better than you think. Your face alone, Debbie, is enough. (RICHARD *kisses her. As* HENRY *begins to pull open her legs,* RICHARD *gets in between. His finger moves gently across her face.*) Eyebrow liners. Mascara. Make-up foundations. Blushers. Skin cleansers. Facial creams. Lipsticks. All kinds of lipsticks. Perfumes. (*Lights fade as* RICHARD *gets on top of* DEBBIE. *The last thing we see is* RANDY *looking on.*)

ACT TWO

SCENE 5

HENNESSY *cottage. Noon.*

Knocking is heard, as the lights come up. JULIE *is gathering up pillows and placing the blanket and pillows to sleep.* ANDREW *appears at the back*

*door. Looks through the curtain. Tries to open the
door. It's closed. He knocks.* JULIE *peeks through
the curtain at* ANDREW. *Not happy to see him.
Opens the door.*

JULIE. What can I do for you, Andrew? (ANDREW *is
amused.*)

ANDREW. That's just what I was going to say. I was
going to say . . . Hello, what can I do for you, Mrs.
Hennessy. Had it all prepared in my head. It was a
toss-up between using, "What can I do for you?" and,
"Top of the morning to you," and I opted for, "What
can I do for you?" because it seemed more professional
and to the point.

JULIE. What is the point, Andrew? Why are you
here?

ANDREW. I'm here because you called me on the telephone.

JULIE. But that was last night. You see . . . when
I called . . . I thought I saw somebody . . .

ANDREW. Why the hell didn't you say so? I mean
. . . you just ring up . . . I pick up and say, "Andrew
here" . . . and you just mutter, "Excuse me," and
hang up. So I dropped by to see why you called me.

JULIE. I just wanted to make sure . . . (*Stops.*)

ANDREW. (*Picks up.*) Oh, I get it. You thought it
was me that was snooping around so you called to
check up on me. Well . . . I was at home . . . so it
wasn't me . . . which can only mean that it was
somebody else.

JULIE. I'm really not sure I saw anybody.

ANDREW. If you'd like I could resume making my
rounds . . . keep an eye on the place.

JULIE. I didn't know you stopped.

ANDREW. I'm just a private security guard and I take my orders from my clients . . . Your husband said not to come around any more while you're up here. Said I made you nervous.

JULIE. You did.

ANDREW. But I don't anymore?

JULIE. I guess not.

ANDREW. So, shall I resume . . . ?

JULIE. Yes. Only don't tell Richard.

ANDREW. Oh, I make him nervous too? Well, I'm glad. I've got a grudge against that man. He's a strange fellow . . . He and that Blackie . . . Saw them swimming in the lake . . . Only reason I can see anybody swimming in that lake is if they want to get dirty. Well . . . Top of the morning to you, Mrs. Hennessy. I know it's not morning but what the hell . . . (*He leaves. Lights go down in the cottage and up on the pier.*)

ACT TWO

SCENE 6

Night. The pier.

RICHARD *and* HENRY *have swum and are now "sunbathing."*

RICHARD. So Henry, want to go for another swim?

HENRY. No. I know why you're a better swimmer than I. They did these tests where it was proven that blacks just don't float as well as whites. In short, we're a race of heavy dudes.

RICHARD. So what do you want to do, Henry?

HENRY. I don't know, Rich. What do you want to do?

RICHARD. I dunno Marty, whaddayou wanna do? Wanna go see a movie or something?

HENRY. What movie?

RICHARD. "The lady in the cottage." We could peek in on the wives and see what they're doing. They do things when they think nobody's looking.

HENRY. I know. I saw Rachel crying once. But then it felt like she knew I was spying on her and did it for my benefit. I can't tell with her. She's got eyes in the back of my head.

RICHARD. I walked into my apartment once and overheard Julie on the telephone . . . she was trying to call up the orphanage where I grew up.

HENRY. Checking up on you.

RICHARD. Yes.

HENRY. I still don't get it. Why would you ever want to make up all that stuff.

RICHARD. Because . . . because, because when I first saw her, Henry, she seemed like some wide-eyed angel who had plopped down from heaven to this cocktail party. There she stood . . . oh, she seemed so spanking sparkling new and unsoiled that I thought I'd love to be like that myself. That it could rub off. I wanted to make a fresh start and share with her something I had never shared with anyone else before. But there was nothing new I could tell her. So I . . . I started making up things . . . a love song to court her with. I created an orphanage where I grew up and populated it with these friends, Aldo and Tee-bone and the rest, who served as mouthpieces for words I was either ashamed or afraid to say on my own. Oh, they were lovely words, Henry. Full of poetry and pathos and unhesitating revelations . . . and I courted her with them. Had she been different she would have caught me at the start. But she was as trusting and openhearted as I made myself out to be . . . and the person she saw in me was far better than the person I really was. It was all based on a lie but in time, I thought, I could recreate myself and become as free and giving as that ghost of the orphanage I had created. It seemed possible. I tried but it got to be so hard. Keeping the ghost alive. Keeping him fed. He turned into a vampire who sucked my soul and imagination dry just to keep going . . . and my life became like some ugly scar that I had to hide. I want to rip of my mask and tell her: Look, Julie, look . . . here I am. But I can't. It would almost be more cruel to do that than . . . I just can't.

HENRY. Oh, man, we've got ourselves in one helluva mess, Rich. So what do we do now?

RICHARD. I don't know, Marty. Whaddayah wanna do? (*He passes the gun to* HENRY.)

HENRY. How long have you had this?

RICHARD. A few months.

HENRY. And do you think you could use it?

RICHARD. I already have.

HENRY. But that was on a dog.

RICHARD. Not when I did it it wasn't.

ACT TWO

SCENE 7

Basketball court. Night.

DEBBIE *and* RANDY *enter talking.*

DEBBIE. I don't know why you keep asking me to tell you when I've already told you everything. I ran and told you right after it happened. The two of them forced me. They held me down and raped me.

RANDY. And you ran and told me right after it happened.

DEBBIE. No, not right after it happened. I had to think. I was afraid. I didn't know what to do.

RANDY. So you thought and you thought and you thought it all over and decided it was rape.

DEBBIE. Of course it was rape. I didn't have to think or decide about that. Why do you say things like that? Don't you believe me?

RANDY. I'm just trying to understand you, Debbie. It's very important that I understand everything.

DEBBIE. What is there to understand?

RANDY. The way you make decisions, Debbie.

DEBBIE. The only decision I made was telling you what happened.

RANDY. Yes, but you waited. And waiting's a decision. I wonder what you thought while you waited.

DEBBIE. What does it matter? It seems that what really matters is that I was raped by the two of them.

RANDY. I've never seen you so angry.

DEBBIE. Of course I'm angry. A thing like that. The bastards. You'd think you'd be angry too.

RANDY. Oh, I'm getting there, Debbie. And they forced you. They held you down and forced you.

DEBBIE. Of course they forced me. What do you think?

RANDY. I wasn't there, Debbie. I don't know what to think. And you called for help?

DEBBIE. I told you I did.

RANDY. Did you shout: Help! Help! Or did you call my name?

DEBBIE. God, how do you expect me to remember . . . I . . . I called your name, I think.

RANDY. Randy! Randy! Is that how you called?

DEBBIE. Yes.

RANDY. Randy? Randy?

DEBBIE. Yes, Randy, Randy.

RANDY. I wish I'd heard you. Had I only heard you calling my name I would have saved you. But then, maybe it's a good thing I didn't. I would have got real angry. I might have hurt them.

DEBBIE. They should be hurt, damnit. They hurt me. They tricked me.

RANDY. Tricked. Not forced?

DEBBIE. Of course they forced me. But they tricked me. I didn't know what they had in mind when they came there. They lied.

RANDY. If there's one thing I hate is that. Liars. And so they raped you?

DEBBIE. How many times do I have to tell you? (RICHARD *enters, takes off his outer clothes and gets under the covers.* JULIE *follows.*)

RANDY. Just a few more so there's no mistake. I mean, each time I made love to you, Debbie, each time, it was like a rape. You made it seem like rape. It wasn't like that, was it?

DEBBIE. My God, do I have to repeat everything ten times!?

RANDY. We all have our own way of making decisions, Debbie. You have your way. I have mine. My way is to hear it over and over again. Because each time you tell me how you were raped, I get a little meaner . . . and when I get mean enough, then I will decide what to do.

DEBBIE. It certainly is taking you a long time.

RANDY. I'm almost there, Debbie. Almost there. (RANDY *exits.*)

DEBBIE. Randy, Randy. (*She calls after him, and exits.*)

ACT TWO

SCENE 8

Everything is the same except that time has passed. It is nearly morning.

RICHARD *and* JULIE *seem to be asleep.* RICHARD'S *arm is hanging off the bed toward the floor.* JULIE *sits up slowly. She looks at* RICHARD.

JULIE. Richard . . . are you awake? (*We see his eyes open and his hand, neither of which she can see, move as a signal that he is awake. The rest of him does not move. She waits a second for a reply.*) I think you are awake but you don't have to say anything. You can pretend you're asleep . . . You can pretend, if you want, that I am a dream you are having . . . it might be better that way because I seem to be unable to say what I want to say when you are looking at me . . . your eyes squint ever so slightly when you look at me . . . as if you were taking aim at my words . . . and all I can do is squirm under your stare and camouflage myself. It's exhausting me, Richard. There is a beautiful life dying inside both of us and it is not in my power to counteract what's happening. It takes energy to break out of this pattern and I just don't have it on my own, Richard. All I seem to want now, my one desire, is to compress all of it . . . all the meals I'll have . . . all the periods, all the lovemaking and the baths and the looks out of the window . . . just compress all of them and get them over with . . . I try. Every morning I want to start anew. I open my eyes and it feels within my power to do so . . . and then I see my slip draped over a chair . . . something sticking out of a drawer . . . my wrist watch is waiting for my wrist, and by the time I put it on it's too late. All these thoughts I am told are not real. I am told there is no soul. I am told there is no God. There are only glands secreting . . . and even the little shred of unhappiness that I thought I could claim as my own . . . even that . . . I am told is nothing more than a case of glands . . . and hormones . . . secreting or undersecreting. I am more than fluids, Richard . . . more . . . I am wounded, I feel, and life is trickling out of me and your lies . . . yes, I know about them . . . your lies will not let the wound heal. I could be a glorious woman. There is so much that is beautiful in me. I beg you, don't keep killing me like this. Let me live. Richard? (*There is only so much as a split second pause and then the alarm clock rings.* RICHARD *sits up as if startled from his sleep. Shuts off the alarm clock. He begins to get dressed.*)

RICHARD. Sleep well, Honey. (*He exits to the basketball court.*)

ACT TWO

SCENE 9

Basketball court. Day.

HENRY *is standing at the free throw line. He's taking careful aim. Shoots. Hit or miss, the ball finally lands on the court and hardly bounces at all. It needs air.* RICHARD *appears.*

(*He walks toward* HENRY. HENRY *is a little nervous. Half whisper.*)

HENRY. Morning, Rich.

RICHARD. Good morning, Henry.

HENRY. Rachel's been in the window for the last hour. She just looks out at me. Look at her.

RICHARD. You don't have to whisper. They can't hear us.

HENRY. I have a feeling they can hear every word.

RICHARD. Just your imagination.

HENRY. I have a feeling they can hear that too.

RICHARD. (*Picks up the ball and "palms" it.*) I have stuffed the ball . . . and I have palmed it . . . my life is full. (*Holding the ball in one hand, he fake-throws it to* HENRY.) It's got to be done soon.

HENRY. I know.

RICHARD. The set-up is getting set up again. Julie will undermine my resolve if it's not done soon.

HENRY. I know. Rachel's at it too. She's telling me how we can make a fresh start . . . forget the past . . . Julie saying that?

RICHARD. Yes.

HENRY. And do you think it's possible?

RICHARD. No.

HENRY. You sure?

RICHARD. Yes.

HENRY. I need you to keep talking.

RICHARD. I just see more lies ahead. Mine. Hers. Ours. I see myself getting older and the more shuffle-stepped I get . . . the more stooped-shouldered and weak-kneed I become, the more she'll tell me, because she knows I'll want to hear it, the more she'll tell me that I'm as vital as ever, no, even more so, that I've improved with age, and wanting to hear such words from a beautiful woman, the more I'll pretend that she too is what she's pretending I am. And we will slosh in that dirty tub of lies until I die and I'll never know . . . not once . . . what it is to be a naked homeless animal . . . free . . . on its own . . .

HENRY. But what happens . . . I mean . . . what do we do after we do it?

RICHARD. I don't know. It's a blank space . . . empty . . . All I know is I yearn for it . . . nobody there in that space to remind me of my potential . . . that goddamned potential . . .

HENRY. Keep talking, Richie, keep feeding me, Baby.

RICHARD. The gun is clean.

HENRY. That's funny. Like we're trying to be neat.

RICHARD. We wipe off the prints . . . throw it somewhere near Andrew's place . . . People have been killed up here before.

HENRY. Is that a legal precedent or something?

RICHARD. You and I were not here when it happened.

HENRY. That's right, Richie, you just keep feeding me.

RICHARD. There's a bar down the road. We were there.

HENRY. Is that it?

RICHARD. No.

HENRY. Good. I want to hear more.

RICHARD. I don't think you can shoot Rachel, Henry. I don't think you can do it.

HENRY. And what am I supposed to say: Yes, I can. I'll show you?

RICHARD. Neither of us can. Not our own. We've lost too many times in front of them.

HENRY. Home court jinx, eh, Richie. So what do we

do? (*A slight pause.* HENRY *doesn't like it.*) No silence, please.

RICHARD. You kill mine and I'll kill yours.

HENRY. That's one up on wife swapping, isn't it? Oh, wow! That's ugly but it sounds better. It sounds like it will be done. It has that sound to it. And so . . . and so . . . who goes first?

RICHARD. We have one last game. Loser goes first.

HENRY. The ball's dead.

RICHARD. No matter. No dribbling. Just shooting. Strictly stuffball. How you get there is your own business.

HENRY. We keep it going. (RICHARD *throws the ball to* HENRY. *It's a weird game they play.* HENRY *carries the ball. No dribbling. It's almost like football except there is no tackling. There is pushing and body checking.* HENRY *runs around trying to fake* RICHARD *out of position so he can stuff dunk. They talk while they play. We can see as much of the game as we want as long as it "plays." They make noises at each other in between the chit chat in order to throw each other off guard. Crowd noises and organ music is heard. Lights fade as the game gets more violent.*)

ACT TWO

SCENE 10

HENNESSY *cottage. Night. The place seems empty.* JULIE *is on the phone as the lights come up.*

JULIE. Rachel . . . I feel funny calling you like this . . . You think I could . . . (*She seems to want to say "come over," but she stops.*) I was just wondering if you knew where the men were . . . I thought maybe. Oh, they're not. (RACHEL *seems to have hung up.* JULIE *puts the phone down. Once again, a certain paralysis seems to be setting into her. She picks up the alarm clock again and plays with the knob until she flicks it in place. The alarm clock rings in her hand until it Stops. She turns and sees* HENRY.) Henry. What're you doing there? (HENRY *appears in view almost on all fours indicating that he had been either lying or sitting there and is now trying to arise.*)

HENRY. Just resting. (*He enters the cottage uninvited. He seems nervous. His face is bruised, his hand is behind his back.*) It was a rough game.

JULIE. Where is Richard?

HENRY. He won. I mean it was a draw. Ten to ten. Eleven to eleven . . . and so on . . . twenty-three all. So we decided to have a sudden death. Free throw wins it. Richie shoots. Richie makes it. Henry gets the ball. And I'm just no good at free throws. You see . . . I just don't have the follow-through . . . it should be natural . . . You just go . . . (*Demonstrates.*) And it's swish . . . but no . . . I could never do it . . . You know . . . just stand there . . . there's no interaction . . . no interplay . . . no pick and roll and give and go, no . . . you just stand there . . . Everything stops. And I don't like that. I like to have some kind of rhythm to carry me through . . . somebody to feed me, you know . . . like guys in my business do one-man shows and things and I just never could . . . I need to have stuff come at me . . . you know . . .

JULIE. Would you like a drink or something?

HENRY. That's the stuff. (*She starts putting ice from a container into a glass. Pours in booze.*)

JULIE. Is Richard out there or what?

HENRY. I don't know. He said . . . What the hell did he say . . . (JULIE *is bringing the drink to* HENRY. *As she turns she sees the gun.*)

JULIE. Isn't that Richard's? (*He stands poised.*)

HENRY. Come on . . . come on, come on . . . say something. You got to speak. I can't do it all. (HENRY *seems like a junkie who needs a fix.*) What kind of goddamned set-up is this? What is this, eh . . . another free throw . . . It doesn't have to be eloquent, you know. Just a couple of lines to play off . . . Shit . . . I know. Phone rings and I play off the ring. Phone rings and I shoot. (*A second or two wait for the phone to ring. Both of them are frozen,* JULIE *crouching with glass of ice cubes in her hand.* HENRY *standing and looking.*) You got a radio? Stereo? Some music or something? (HENRY *is really getting frantic. He stops suddenly.*) That was just preparation. Here it comes. Score's all tied up. In bounds pass. The clock doesn't start til he gets the ball. In bounds pass to Henry . . . (*He "dribbles" towards the exit.*) He dribbles . . . he drives . . . he stops . . . shoots. (*He shoots twice and then exits.* JULIE *stands.*)

ACT TWO

SCENE 11

RICHARD *is waiting at the pier.* HENRY *runs out of the cottage. He stumbles past the basketball court, gun in hand. He seems out of control.* RICHARD *is tense and excited at the same time.* HENRY *staggers toward him.*

RICHARD. I heard the shots.

HENRY. How'd they sound?

RICHARD. Well?

HENRY. Yes?

RICHARD. Did you do it?

HENRY. What do you think?

RICHARD. You did it?

HENRY. Is that what you think?

RICHARD. C'mon. C'mon. Did-you-do-it!?

HENRY. You heard the shots.

RICHARD. Is she dead?

HENRY. Not unless she keeled over from a heart attack.

RICHARD. HENRY. This is not time for games, dammit.

HENRY. Black man speak with dry tongue. (RICHARD *is getting frantic.*)

RICHARD. HENRY! (*Gestures as if to come after him with his hands.* HENRY *counters by pointing the pistol at him.*)

HENRY. You better watch it. I've missed with this baby once and I can miss again. (*Laughs at his own despair.* RICHARD *realizes.*)

RICHARD. You didn't kill her.

HENRY. Kill her! I couldn't strike up a conversation with her.

RICHARD. Oh, Christ.

HENRY. A clutch shot at the buzzer. And I blew it. We're into overtime.

RICHARD. Shut up with that stuff.

HENRY. But there's no such thing as a miss, right? I get a quarter point.

RICHARD. Will you drop that stuff. I'm trying to think. I got to do something.

HENRY. It was terrible. She killed the scene. She said nothing. Nothing. She just played with these ice cubes. I got nervous and started chattering. It was like a blind date. You'd think I was trying to get a good night kiss from her.

RICHARD. WHAT THE HELL DID YOU SHOOT FOR THEN?

HENRY. TO END THE SCENE. TO GET MY-SELF TO SHUT UP. It was terrible. It's like she knew I couldn't do it and felt sorry for me.

RICHARD. Why couldn't you do it?

HENRY. Because I was by myself. You should've sent me in there with that transistor radio. We could've listened to some music. Had some potato chips.

RICHARD. Listen to me. Listen. Nothing's lost. There's just a change of plans.

HENRY. I can't take no more plans. Let's raise the rim, Rich. The damned thing feels like it's around my neck. I can't think straight with that thing . . .

RICHARD. Calm down. Just calm down. It's not too late. Do you understand?

HENRY. Let's raise it so high, so damned high, that we don't even consider it. Oh, God, it's like she knew I couldn't do it and felt sorry for me.

RICHARD. She tricked you. Do you understand? She tricked you.

HENRY. It was some trick. She had an ice cube. I had a gun. She won.

RICHARD. All right. Forget everything, Henry. You stay here. Just give me the gun.

HENRY. I'm staying nowhere by myself.

RICHARD. Give the gun.

HENRY. If you could've done it you would have by now.

RICHARD. I killed that dog, didn't I? (HENRY *cracks up*.)

HENRY. Killed the dog. Oh, that's rich, all right. Well, I've drowned a few goldfish in my time too. (*He can't keep his eyes off the cottage.*) Look. Her lights are still off. Hey, maybe she went to bed. Eh, wouldn't that be something. Goes to bed. Leaves you a note. Rich: Dinner's in the oven. (RICHARD *switches tactics in mid course. It does no good to assault* HENRY. *So he tries something else.*)

RICHARD. That would be like her.

HENRY. They got our number, Rich.

RICHARD. They sure do, Henry.

HENRY. Tomorrow morning it'll be like nothing happened. It'll be sleep well dear?

RICHARD. I guess you're right. (*He tries to be casual but his eagerness is showing.*) Might as well give me that thing.

HENRY. What do you want the "thing" for.

RICHARD. Well, it's my "thing" isn't it? (*The strain is showing on* RICHARD.)

HENRY. We're getting a divorce, eh? Well, I'll let you visit the little rascal on weekends.

RICHARD. Please, Henry. Eh? C'mon. Give me the gun.

HENRY. Let's throw it away.

RICHARD. Listen to me, Henry. Listen to me, please. I can't go back to her. She'll forgive me. I can't take to be forgiven. It nullifies you. She'll understand me and I can't take to be understood anymore. I feel I can do it. And I know myself well enough to know that the feeling won't last. It will go away and another feeling will take its place. I have to hurry. I have to do it now.

HENRY. What about me?

RICHARD. You're free to do what you want.

HENRY. I'm not asking for permission. I'm asking for an answer. (RICHARD *loses control.*)

RICHARD. Give me the gun, damn you.

HENRY. You can't kill her.

RICHARD. I can do it.

HENRY. Well I can't! So I'd like to think nobody can. I got to have company in this world. I'm throwing the damned thing in the lake.

RICHARD. You can't! (HENRY *tries to go to the pier to hurl the gun in the lake.* RICHARD *intercepts him and goes for the gun. They struggle. As they do* RANDY *appears behind them with a rifle.* HENRY *and* RICHARD's *physical struggle becomes* RANDY's *internal struggle. He's not sure he can do it. For a second or two he seems ready to give up and leave. At this moment* RICHARD *overpowers* HENRY. *Takes the gun from him.* HENRY's *still clinging to him.* RICHARD *tries to free himself and as he does the gun in his hand seems to swing toward* RANDY's *direction.* RANDY *plays off their action. Fires once. Fires twice.* HENRY *and* RICHARD *fall into the boathouse.*)

ACT TWO

SCENE 12

Basketball court. Night.

RACHEL *is* U. C. *on the court.* ANDREW *talks to* RACHEL. RANDY *and* DEBBIE *are* D. R.

ANDREW. Randy said they had a gun and were going to force his girl to do something. I don't see why he'd lie. He hardly knew them. So that's what I'll tell the police unless there's something you know that I don't know that you'd like me to know.

RACHEL. It's a terrible shock to both of us.

ANDREW. That I know. You want me to arrange for some transportation for you.

RACHEL. No, thank you. My friend here will drive me.

ANDREW. Fine. Good night. (*He crosses* D. S. *to* RANDY *and takes his gun.*) If the police asks why you had the gun you tell them you were making the rounds for me. Hear?

RANDY. Yes, Uncle. (ANDREW *walks on.*)

DEBBIE. You said you were just going to frighten them. You swore you wouldn't shoot.

RANDY. But I did. And you brought me the gun.

DEBBIE. You asked me to do it.

RANDY. And you asked me to do it.

DEBBIE. Not to kill.

RANDY. Did you say that?

DEBBIE. No, but it was understood.

RANDY. You brought me the gun, Debbie.

DEBBIE. You asked me to do it.

RANDY. You didn't have to, Debbie.

DEBBIE. You said you were just going to scare them. Teach them a lesson.

RANDY. Yes, but then I remembered how they raped you. How they forced you. How you called my name. Randy. Randy. And I lost control.

DEBBIE. I don't believe you.

RANDY. I believe everything you tell me.

DEBBIE. Why does it all keep coming back to me.

RANDY. I did it because of you. Because of what they did to you. And you brought me the gun, Debbie.

DEBBIE. Stop saying that.

RANDY. I said you'll have to bring me the gun, Debbie. I said, Uncle keeps it in his room and he won't let me into his room. But he'll let you. I said, pretend you're going into his room to use the big mirror and then lower the gun through the window. And you did. While Uncle and I talked in the living room you went in there and lowered the gun and then you came out. Both of us saw you. Uncle knows what you did. But you don't have to worry about anything, Debbie. We'll cover up for you. I was making the rounds. I came upon them trying to rape you and I shot them. You're in the clear.

DEBBIE. Oh. That's right. You see . . . you had me worried the way you talked . . .

RANDY. You have absolutely nothing to worry about.

DEBBIE. Yes, and I'll go home in a few days. I mean as soon as . . .

RANDY. You are home, Debbie.

DEBBIE. What are you talking about.

RANDY. You can't leave me now. You have to stand by your man.

DEBBIE. You couldn't be more wrong.

RANDY. I could be more of everything, Debbie.

DEBBIE. I'm going to leave tonight. (DEBBIE *moves away.*)

RANDY. Then I might have to tell the police about the gun.

DEBBIE. Please, Randy . . . please let me go.

RANDY. But you don't want to go, Debbie. You've tried it once already. (*He leads her away by the arm. She is too weak to resist.* JULIE *enters from the house.*)

RACHEL. How are you feeling?

JULIE. I don't know. It's like I don't dare feel anything.

RACHEL. Of course. It's a terrible shock. Losing your husband like that. At least you're not alone. I'll stay with you as long as you need me.

JULIE. Nobody ever wanted to hurt me like that. I turned around and there he was with a gun in his hand. I still remember the way he looked at me.

RACHEL. Forget about Henry.

JULIE. It was Richard.

RACHEL. You must calm down. You're getting all confused.

JULIE. I saw him.

RACHEL. You saw Henry.

JULIE. I saw Henry come in and then when I turned around I saw Richard standing in front of me with a gun in his hand. I was paralyzed. Now they're dead!

RACHEL. It had nothing to do with us. Nobody forced them to do anything.

JULIE. (*Crosses* D. R.) But we followed along and by doing that we forced them to lead.

RACHEL. You want to take all the blame.

JULIE. No, just my share. (*Sits.*)

RACHEL. Nobody has to know about this. About us . . . It can be our little secret.

JULIE. I've kept too many secrets. I don't want to do it anymore.

RACHEL. (*She wheels* D. S.) Listen to me, Julie. We all have those women in us . . . tender little things . . . and we all want to let them out for the world to see . . . but the world kills them, Julie. Men smell the victim on you. Hide the scent. Change before it's too late.

JULIE. I think I've changed too much already and left something essential behind. I feel so transparent.

I can see all my joints and seams but the framework is there. I can almost touch it.

RACHEL. Aren't we going back together?

JULIE. There is a way out of this pattern and I must find it on my own.

CURTAIN

PROPERTY LIST

ACT ONE

PRESET: on stage

couch with 4 blue pillows and dustcover, windows closed, table tucked away, chairs under, clock on bookcase, 3 or more glasses on shelf, 3 cups, hanging spoon ready on counter, pitcher of water, empty coffeepot and dishes U. S., yogurt in fridge and some jars on shelf, telephone, telephone book and photo album, yellow towel in towel ring, rim at 10′ mark, bench S. L. of door on U. L. house, boathouse door open, purse on D. S. end of couch

S. L.

leather basketball, paint can with water, brush and rag, wheelchair in U. L. house, grocery bag with flyswatter, large green suitcase, attache with loaded gun, straw purse, shotgun and one live shell

S. R.

roll of toilet paper with tape, stack of books, handkerchief and blood, flashlight, bottle of perfume, handbag, "Andrew's" blank shells, yoga book and tape cassette with tape cued up, radio folded in yellow towel

ACT TWO (underlined items may be set at top of show but must be checked at inter)

PRESET:

coffee in pot, ice in bowl in freezer, O.J. on shelf, in fridge, table with U. S. leaf up and D. S. L. leg on mark, 2 cups, 2 glasses O.J. (1 slightly one-third), 1 plate with three-quarters of sandwich and jar of jam, window closed, alarm on book case set to go off (strike: flyswatter, attache, tape and yoga bench reset)

S. L.

2 basketballs, fake gun, shotgun, beige towel and baby oil, wheelchair on platform by speaker

S. R.

bed pillow and blanket (brown), clock set to ring behind s. R. wall of s. R. house